D1269924

FIRST THEATER IN AMERICA

Charles P. Daly L.L.D.

Chief Judge of the New York Common Pleas.
President of the American Geographical Society &c.

FIRST THEATER IN AMERICA

WHEN WAS THE DRAMA
FIRST INTRODUCED IN AMERICA?

An Inquiry

BY

HON. CHARLES P. DALY, LL. D.

INCLUDING

A CONSIDERATION OF THE OBJECTIONS THAT HAVE BEEN
MADE TO THE STAGE

KENNIKAT PRESS, INC./PORT WASHINGTON, N. Y.

FIRST THEATER IN AMERICA

First published 1896
Reissued 1968 by Kennikat Press

Library of Congress Catalog Card No: 68-26284
Manufactured in the United States of America

INTRODUCTION.

The paper here reprinted by the Dunlap Society was read before the New York Historical Society more than thirty years ago. In looking through the files of Colonial newspapers in the possession of that institution for another purpose, my attention was called by the late Thomas F. De Voe, who devoted his leisure largely to the examination of Colonial newspapers, and especially those of Colonial New York, to an advertisement showing that there was a theater in the City of New York anterior to the arrival of the company that, as Dunlap expressed it, "planted the drama in America." I followed up Mr. De Voe's discovery by going over the Colonial newspapers of New York in the possession of the Historical Society for further information, and embodied the result in the paper read before that body. The paper was published at the time in the "New York Evening Post," and a limited number of copies of it were printed by that journal in pamphlet form. In expressing a wish to reprint it the Dunlap Society requested that I would augment the information by an account of what has since been ascertained upon the subject, a request with which I have complied by adding it at the end as a supplement, preferring that the paper should remain as it appeared originally.

NEW·YORK

FOUNDED IN

MDCCCLXXXV

THE DUNLAP SOCIETY

First Theater in America.

WHEN WAS THE DRAMA
FIRST INTRODUCED IN AMERICA?

DUNLAP, the historian of the American Stage, informs us that the drama was introduced in this country by William Hallam, the successor of Garrick in Goodman's Field Theatre, who formed a joint stock company and sent them to America under the management of his brother Lewis Hallam in the year 1752, and that the first play ever acted in America was the "Merchant of Venice," represented by this company on September 5, 1752, at Williamsburg, then the capital of Virginia, in an old store-house which they converted into a theater within two months after their arrival at Yorktown. Dunlap's familiarity with the subject, the fact that he derived his information from Lewis Hallam, Jr., who came out a boy twelve years of age with this early company, and the circumstance that Burke, in his "History of Virginia," has the same statement, have been deemed sufficiently satisfactory, and William Hallam, whom Dunlap calls

" the Father of the American stage," has been accepted as the person who first introduced the drama in America.*

THE FIRST THEATER IN NEW YORK.

BUT Dunlap and those upon whom he relied were mistaken, for there was a theater in the city of New York in 1733, nineteen years before Hallam arrived in this country. It is mentioned in Bradford's " Gazette " of that year, in the advertisement of a merchant who directs inquiries to be made of him at his store

---

*This is a mistake. Dunlap gives a quotation from Burke's "History of Virginia " as follows : " Under the presidency of Thomas Lee, the New York Company of Comedians obtained permission to erect a theatre in Williamsburg, *i. e.*, in the year 1750, when no New York company existed, or any other on the continent." The last sentence, "when no New York company existed, or any other on the continent," is not by Burke, but by Dunlap, which led me to suppose that Burke agreed with Dunlap that the drama was first introduced in America by Hallam. Burke refers to Kean & Murray's company, who played in New York from the 6th of March to the 30th of April, 1750, and in the subsequent part of the year may have gone to Williamsburg, Virginia, and obtained permission to erect a theater there as stated by Burke.* Dunlap afterward acknowledged his error in a manuscript note to his copy of his history, now in the possession of Thomas J. McKee, Esq., of the city of New York.

Burke's "History of Virginia," Vols. i and ii.   Harpers, 1832.

"next door to the Play-House." * This reference is all that has been found respecting it; but in the month of February, 1750, more than two years before the arrival of Hallam, a regular company of actors, under the joint management of Thomas Kean and of a Mr. Murray, came to this city from Philadelphia, and applied to Admiral George Clinton, then the governor of the Province of New York, for permission to act. Governor Clinton was a man of rank, the son of an earl, and had previously held a distinguished position as commander of the English fleet in the Mediterranean, while his wife, Lady Clinton, was a woman of great personal attractions and very agreeable manners, who had moved in the first circles of London society. To these cultivated persons there was nothing objectionable in the establishment of a theater, and permission was accordingly granted, though, from the spirit afterward exhibited by the local magistrates in this and other places, it would probably have been refused had the city authorities been applied to. It was announced through the columns of the "Weekly Post Boy" that the company intended to perform as long as the season lasted, provided they met with suitable encouragement, and upon obtaining the consent of

---

* The advertisement is as follows : " To be Sold at reasonable Rates, All Sorts of Household Goods, viz., Beds, Chairs, Tables, Chests of Drawers, Looking Glasses, Andirons, and Pictures as also several sorts of Druggs and Medicines, also a Negro Girl about 16 years of age, has had the Small-pox and is fit for Town or Country. Enquire of *George Talbot*, next Door to the Play-House."—"New York Gazette," October 15, 1733.

the governor they hired a large room in a building in Nassau street, belonging to the estate of Rip Van Dam, formerly president of the Provincial Council, and converted it into a theater; and here, on March 5, 1750, they produced Shakespeare's historical play of "Richard III.," as altered by Colley Cibber, in which the part of *Richard* was performed by Mr. Kean. The performance was announced to begin precisely at half-past seven o'clock, and the public were informed that no person would be admitted behind the scenes — an important reform, as it had been the practice in London from Shakespeare's time to allow the purchasers of box tickets free access to the stage; a custom which led to many abuses and immoralities.

CAPACITY OF THE THEATER.

THE room which had been converted into a theater must have been a very capacious one, as it was arranged with pit and gallery, and afterward boxes were added. The price of admission to the boxes was eight shillings, to the pit five shillings, and to the gallery three shillings. The exact capacity of this theater is known from the following circumstances: Upon the occasion of Mr. Kean's benefit, who was the leading tragedian, he was honored by a crowded house in his favorite part of *Richard III.*, and great complaint having been made that more tickets had been sold than the house could hold, Kean published a card in the " Post Boy," which was accompanied by a certificate of Parker, the publisher, to the effect that he had printed in all 161 pit tickets, 10 box, and 121 gallery tickets, declaring that as great a number had been in the house before. Kean in his card informs the public that it had been determined not to receive any money at the door, but that it was impossible to carry out that intention without giving great offense, and that the purchasers of tickets who had come after the house was filled had had their money returned. It may be inferred from this circumstance that the players found " satisfactory encouragement." " Richard III." appears to have been a favorite piece, and on March 12, 1750, it was announced that it would be acted for the last time, together with the farce of " The Beau in the Suds," and that on the following Saturday Dryden's play of " The Spanish Friar" would be represented. They continued to play on Monday, Wednesday, and Saturday from the 5th of March to the 30th of April, 1750, when the season closed, and that the experiment was successful may be inferred from the fact that they opened the theater again for another season on the 30th of December, 1750, and continued to play three times a week until the 17th of June, 1751, closing with a succession of benefits, when the company went to Virginia.

CHANGE OF MANAGEMENT.

BEFORE the close of the season, Kean, the joint manager, withdrew, announcing in a formal card to the public that he had resolved to quit the stage, by the advice of several gentlemen in town who were his friends, and follow his employment of writing; that his co-manager, Mr. Murray, had agreed to give him a night clear of all expenses for his half of the clothes and scenery of the playhouse, and that by his Excellency the Governor's permission he would, on the following Monday evening, enact the part of *King Richard III.* for his benefit, being the last time of his appearance upon the stage. On the Monday following, April 29, 1751, the performance for his benefit was changed to "The Busybody" and "The Virgin Unmasked," and in announcing the change he informs the public, as an additional attraction, that there will be singing by Mr. Woodham, and particularly the celebrated ode called "Britons' Charter," closing with this appeal: "As this will positively be the last time of Mr. Kean's appearing upon the stage, he honestly hopes all gentlemen and ladies, and others who are his well wishers, will be so kind as to favor him with their company."

PLAYS PRODUCED.

HOW this company were collected, or where they originally came from, it is probably now no longer possible to ascertain. As they were announced, upon their first appearance in New York, as a company of comedians who had come from Philadelphia, it is highly probable that they had played before in the Southern cities, and that they came originally from the West Indies, where, especially in Jamaica, theatrical companies from England had been in the habit of performing for some years previously. During the two seasons of the company in New York the following plays were given: "Richard III."; Otway's "Orphan"; Dryden's "Spanish Friar"; Farquhar's "Sir Harry Wildair," being the sequel to the "Trip to the Jubilee"; "Recruiting Officer" and "Beaux' Stratagem"; "George Barnwell"; "The Beggar's Opera"; "The Distressed Mother"; Congreve's "Love for Love" and the "Bold Stroke for a Wife"; with the following farces: "The Beau in the Suds," "The Mock Doctor," "The Devil to Pay," "The Walking Statue," "The Old Man Taught Wisdom," "Damon and Phillida," "Hob in the Well," and "Miss in Her Teens." The names of the *dramatis personæ* were not printed in the play-bills, for the reason, probably, that the same actor had to play different parts in the same piece, but from references made to individual performers, the following persons are known to have been members of the company: Kean and Murray, the joint managers;

Messrs. Taylor, Woodham, Tremaine, Jago, Scott, Moore, Marks, and Master Dickey Murray, the manager's son; Miss Nancy George, Miss Osborne, Mrs. Taylor, Mrs. Davis, and Mrs. Osborne. Kean, Tremaine, and Jago played in tragic parts. Murray and Taylor were comedians. Miss Nancy George and Miss Osborne were the chief ladies in comedy and tragedy. Woodham and Mrs. Taylor were comedians and vocalists, and Kean, like his more distinguished namesake, Edmund Kean, appears to have possessed some musical talent, for on the occasion of his first benefit he announces that he will sing " an oratorio." Master Dickey Murray would seem to have been a favorite of the public. The other actors performed in subordinate parts.

CURIOUS ANNOUNCEMENTS.

DURING the second season, which lasted for six months, they had repeated the same plays many times, and probably having nothing new or more attractive to offer for another season, they determined to try their fortunes elsewhere. They closed with a series of benefits, and some of the appeals made respecting them are sufficiently curious to be noticed. Mrs. Davis announces that a benefit is given to her to enable her to buy off her time, and she hopes that all ladies and gentlemen who are charitably inclined will favor

it, closing in legal phraseology, " and their humble pe-
titioner, as in duty bound, will ever pray." It was the
constant practice at that time for masters of vessels to
bring out passengers to New York upon the condition
that they should be sold immediately upon their arrival
as servants to any person who would pay their passage-
money. They were sold for a definite period of time and
were called Redemptioners, of which class Mrs. Davis,
from her earnest appeal, appears to have been one.
Mr. Jago humbly begs that all gentlemen and ladies
will be so kind as to favor him with their company, as
he never had a benefit before, and *is just come out of
prison ;* and Mrs. Osborne appropriately selects the
play of " The Distressed Mother," with the announcement that it is the first time this poor widow has had a
benefit, and having met with divers late hardships and
misfortunes she appeals to the benevolent and *others.*

It is stated in Clapp's " Records" that Otway's
" Orphan " was played in Boston, in the Coffee House
in State street, in the early part of 1750, by two young
Englishmen, assisted by some volunteer comrades of
the town; and as this is about the period when Murray
& Kean's company began to perform in New York,
this may possibly have been an initiatory attempt on
the part of some of the members of that company to
introduce dramatic amusements among the people of
New England. Whether it was so or not, it was immediately followed by the passage of an act by the
General Court of Massachusetts, in March, 1750, pro-
hibiting stage plays and theatrical entertainments of
any kind.

A NEW COMPANY IN 1751.

IN the winter of 1751 another company came to New York, and opened the theater in Nassau street on December 23, 1751, with "Othello" and the farce of "Lethe." The company was under the management of a Mr. Upton, and in all probability came from Jamaica, in a vessel which had arrived a short time before. The company were either inferior to the former, or the public had become indifferent, for the manager, after performing three weeks, announced that, to his great disappointment, he had not met with encouragement enough to support the company for the season, and that he would bring it to an end by giving a few benefits. Some doubt of the merits of the new performers seems to have prevailed, as he assured the public in a card that the company "were perfect, and hope to perform to satisfaction." It was the custom then for the actors to wait upon all the principal inhabitants and solicit their patronage, and fearing that he had been held accountable for some remissness of duty in this particular, he begs the public to remember that "he is an absolute stranger in the city, and if in his application he has omitted any gentlemen or ladies' house or lodging, he humbly hopes that they will impute it to his want of information, and not to want of respect." But though he produced several pieces not yet played in New York, such as "The Fair Penitent," "Venice Preserved," "The Provoked Husband," and "Othello," it was of no avail. A few benefits were given, one for a Mr. Leigh, another one for the poor widow Osborne, who, with Mr. Tremaine of the former company, had become attached to this one; and on March 27, 1752, the last performance took place for the benefit of the manager's wife, Mrs. Upton. Upton delivered a farewell epilogue, and a few days after he left in a vessel for London.

THE DRAMA IN VIRGINIA AND MARYLAND.

THE prior company, after performing in Virginia, went to Annapolis, the capital of Maryland, and erected a small theater there, which they opened on June 22, 1752, with "The Beggar's Opera," and the farce of "The Lying Valet." Annapolis was at this period a place of considerable trade and commerce, with a thriving population, including many wealthy merchants, and being the capital of the province, was the residence of the leading officials, and a general place of resort for opulent planters and their families. There was among the people a great deal of refinement and cultivation. They were much more disposed to enjoy the recreation of the theater than the mixed English, French, and Dutch population of New York, and consequently the theater there was a permanent institution, and continued to be so for many years. The company represented the same plays which they had before acted in New York, with the addition of "Cato" and "The Busybody"; and after playing for a season they gave representations in other parts of Maryland. Some new names appear among the members, such as Eyrarson, Wynell, and Herbert, while many of the old members had left, a circumstance warranting the supposition that there was either another company then performing in the South, or that these actors had returned to England or to the West Indies. Among the remaining members were Murray, Scott, and Miss Osborne; and Kean, despite his formal farewell in New York, and declaration of his intention to resume his original occupation of a writing-master, was again among them, representing principal parts.

All that has been here narrated occurred before Hallam came to this country and gave his first representation at Williamsburg, Virginia, in the autumn of 1752. He afterward went to Annapolis, and in the summer of 1753 he came with his company to New York. Finding the old theater in Nassau street inadequate to his purpose, he took the building down and erected upon the same spot what the newspaper of the day, Parker's "Gazette," describes "as a very fine, large, and commodious new theater," which he opened on September 17, 1753, with Steele's comedy of "The Conscious Lovers" and the farce of "Damon and Phillida." Dunlap says that it was erected on the spot afterward occupied by the old Dutch Church (the present post-office). In this he was also mistaken, for the church was on the place where the building now stands in 1729. The theater which Hallam built, and the one before it, were on the east side of Nassau street, between Maiden lane and John street.

HALLAM'S THEATER IN NASSAU STREET.

HALLAM'S company was far superior to any that preceded it. Mrs. Hallam was not only a beautiful woman, but she was an actress of no ordinary merit. Dunlap in his youth heard old ladies speak in raptures of her beauty, grace, and pathos. Hallam was himself an excellent comedian, and two other members of the company, Rigby and Malone, were actors of established reputation upon the London boards. The arrival of a complete company like this, who were not only practised in their art but amply provided before their departure with dresses, and all that was necessary for effective dramatic representation, was something too formidable to contend against. They seem, therefore, to have entirely supplanted the earlier pioneers, of whom nothing further is known except that some of their number, Murray, Tremaine, Scott, and Miss Osborne, played in Hallam's original company afterward, when it was under the management of Douglass.

After performing in New York for the winter, Hallam went with his company to Philadelphia in April,

1754, and from there to the West Indies, where he died. In 1758 the company returned to New York, under the management of Douglass, who had married Hallam's widow. During the four years that they had been absent the theater remained unoccupied, and a short time before their arrival a congregation of German Calvinists had ben formed, and being in want of a place of worship they purchased the theater in Nassau street for $1250, and fitted it up as a church, which they continued to occupy until 1765, when the building, which had not been a very substantial one, becoming decayed, they took it down and erected, upon the spot, another edifice, which was standing fifteen years ago, and was familiarly known as Gosling's Eating House, Nos. 64 and 66 Nassau street.

Finding that the theater had been converted into a church, Douglass built another one upon Cruger's Wharf, a large pier, with houses upon it, which at that time extended from Pearl street into the East River, between Old and Coenties slips. In the following year, 1759, Douglass went to Philadelphia, where he erected a small theater, and from there to Annapolis, where he built a very fine one of brick, capable of accommodating between five and six hundred people, which he opened March 3, 1760.

THE BEEKMAN STREET THEATER.

IN 1761 Douglass returned to New York, and abandoning the theater upon Cruger's Wharf, erected one in Beekman street, a few doors below Nassau street. This was torn down in a riot in 1764. Three years after, the theater in John street, between Nassau street and Broadway, was built, which continued to be the principal one until the erection of the old Park Theater in 1797.*

* It was in 1766 and not in 1764 that this theater in Beekman street, or, as it was then called, Chapel street, was torn down in a riot growing out of the Stamp Act. The bill for the performance that night was " May 5, 1766, at the theatre in Chapel Street, a comedy called the 'Twin Rivals,' with a Song in praise of liberty and the King and the Miller of Mansfield.

" N. B. As the packet is arrived and has been the messenger of good news relative to the Repeal it is hoped the public has no objection to the above performance "— a hope that was not fulfilled.

Gabriel Furman, in a manuscript history of the New York stage, says, " about the year 1761 Phil Miller, well-known in the city for a plodding, active, managing man, obtained permission of Governor Colden to build a theatre and act plays, which he did in Beekman Street, a little below Nassau Street. This was a wooden building, in poor condition, with paper scenery and a wretched wardrobe. The whole was destroyed by a mob, created by the Stamp Act. Phil Miller lost his house and company. He was a jocose fellow and played Justice Gattle with great humor."

SUPPLEMENT.

VERY early information respecting the drama in North America is found in a letter by Chief Justice Samuel Sewall of Massachusetts, dated March 2, 1714, in which he protests against the acting of a play in the Council Chamber at Boston, affirming that even the Romans, fond as they were of plays, were not "so far set upon them as to turn their Senate House into a Play-House." "Let not Christian Boston," he continues, "goe beyond Heathen Rome in the practice of Shamefull Vanities."

Some account of this early opponent of the American drama may not be out of place here, as he was an interesting character. He was born in England and came to New England with his parents, who settled in Newbury, Massachusetts. After graduating at Harvard College he entered the ministry, which vocation he left after a short time and took charge of the printing-press in Boston, which was under his management for three years. He had also other public trusts. He was a member of the Council, a judge of the Court of Probates, and afterward became Chief Justice of Massachusetts. As a judge he took part in what is known as the Salem Witchcraft Trials, and is said to have been the only one of the judges who publicly confessed his error. In 1697, five years after these trials, he prepared a written confession, which was read to the congregation of the old South Church in Boston by the minister, the judge, during the reading, standing up in his place, and during the remaining thirty-one years of his life he spent one day annually in fasting, meditation, and prayer, to keep in mind a sense of the enormity of his offense.   This public exhibition of remorse was what might be expected on the part of a truly conscientious man, for the drama to which he was so much opposed has not often been used for the fictitious representation of scenes more harrowing than those he witnessed and took part in in Salem; scenes that find their counterpart to-day only among the superstitious savages of Western Africa.

The minister of the church in the village of Salem, who had had a bitter strife with a portion of his congregation, got up this accusation of witchcraft, as a means of vengeance in which he was both accuser and witness, prompting the answers of other witnesses and acting as recorder to the magistrates, in which he was supported throughout by Cotton Mather.   Within less than two months twenty persons were tried, condemned, and hanged, among them five women of blameless lives, all declaring their innocence.   A minister was hanged as a witch for declaring that there could be no such thing as witchcraft, " an opinion," says Bancroft, that " wounded the self-love of the judges, for it made them the accusers and judicial murderers of the innocent."   Fifty-five persons were tortured or terrified into confession.   " With accusations," continues the historian, " confessions increased, and with confessions new accusations."   The jails were full.   No one that confessed after condemnation was hanged, but those who retracted after confession were. A minister of the gospel is recorded as saying : " There hang eight firebrands of hell ! " pointing to the bodies swinging on the gallows,* and the writer of a production which exposed the whole proceeding to ridicule, and was chiefly instrumental in putting an end to it, was denounced as " a coal from hell " by Cotton Mather, who, through religious vanity, credulity, self-righteousness, ambition, or all combined, while he ceased subsequently to repeat the statements or accusations, unlike Sewall, made no acknowledgment thereafter of his error.

This striking example of judicial conscientiousness on the part of Sewall was not a single characteristic of this Puritan chief justice, for in addition to being an able man, he was also a benevolent one, whose warmest sympathies were with the down-trodden and oppressed. In 1700 he published a tract entitled "The Selling of Joseph," in which he advocated the rights of the slaves in the Colonies, and to that extent may be regarded as one of the pioneers in this country in the long struggle for negro emancipation. He was the author of several publications upon religious subjects, and of one upon the Kennebec Indians, but at the present day is chiefly known for a diary published by the Massachusetts Historical Society that he kept during the larger part of his life, which, in addition to being entertaining, sheds much light upon the manners, habits, and social state of New England at that period.

* 3 Bancroft's " History," n. s., chap. 19.

It may fairly be assumed that what he protested against did not take place, for if the play had been acted in the Council Chamber some account of it or reference to it would, in all probability, have come down to us.

While preparing my former paper I met with certain statements that satisfied me that English actors had been in the West Indies by whom plays had been performed there, but at how early a period, or whether they or any of them had come to the North American colonies and had been members of the companies referred to in the paper, I had not been able to ascertain, but I afterwards found that it appears by a Barbadoes newspaper of March 18, 1731, that in 1728 some gentlemen in Barbadoes acted plays, the names of Mr. Vaughan and Mr. Rice being given; the former of whom delivered a prologue and the latter an epilogue; I was also disposed to think that in 1732 they had a theater there, for it appeared by a news-paper of that year that on August 16, 1732, "The Royal Consort" was acted, that the prologue was spoken by a Mr. John Snow, and the epilogue would appear by a Miss Whiten, who are referred to as new comers to the island.*

Mr. Thomas J. McKee, of the city of New York, however, possesses a small quarto volume, now extremely rare, published in the eighteenth century by Anthony Aston, or, as he was generally known, Tony Aston, who had been an actor in the West Indies and

* "Caribbeana," Vol i, p. 380.   London, 1741.

afterward came to Virginia and New York, who, according to his own statement, acted in the city of New York in 1702. He may have been one of those who were to act the play referred to by Chief Justice Sewall in the Boston Council Chamber in 1714, but it will not be necessary to dwell further here upon this information or indulge in any conjectures respecting it, as Mr. McKee has written a paper upon Aston and his career, which is to be published by the Dunlap Society.

The first representation, in North America, of a play, as far as known, occurred in 1718 in Williamsburg, then the capital of Virginia. It is mentioned in a letter by Governor Spottiswood dated June 24, 1718. Spottiswood was governor of Virginia from 1710 to 1722, and though popular with the people is described as " imperious and contemptuous," characteristics which, no doubt, led to what he details in the letter in which he refers to this theatrical performance, characteristics which may have been justified if, as he said in one of his letters, " the people had elected to the House of Burgesses a set of representatives whom Heaven has not generally endowed with the ordinary qualifications requisite in legislators, and who placed at the head of standing committees men who could neither spell English, nor write common sense."

In this letter of June 24, 1718, he refers to eight members of the House of Assembly, who slighted an invitation to his house at an entertainment that he gave. He could not prevail upon any one of them to pay him " the common compliment of a visit, when," he writes, "in order to the solemnizing His Majesty's birthday, I gave a public entertainment at my house, and all gentlemen that would come were admitted, these eight committeemen would neither come to my house nor go *to the play which was acted on the occasion*," but on the contrary, he says, "these eight committeemen got together all the turbulent and disappointed burghers to an entertainment of their own in the House of Burgesses, and invited the mob, and plentifully supplied it with liquor, to drink the same health as was drunk in the governor's house, taking no more notice of the governor than if there had been none in the place."*

What this play was or when it was performed does not appear, but where it was acted may be conjectured, as will subsequently appear.

Graham in his "History of the United States of North America," published in London in 1736,† in describing Williamsburg, the capital of Virginia, in the early part of the eighteenth century, says that "it contained a theater for dramatic performances, *the first institution of the kind in the British* colonies." He does not state from what source he obtained this information, but as he quotes a passage from a work entitled "The Present State of Virginia," by Hugh Jones, published in London in 1724, "the substance of which," he states, "is embraced in the second volume of Oldmixon's British Colonies," he probably knew noth-

* Spottiswood's Letters, collections of the Virginia Historical Society, Vol. ii, p. 284.

† "History of the United States of North America," Vol. iii, p. 146, 147 : London, 1836.

ing respecting this theater except what he found in Oldmixon. Rich, the bibliographer, says that Jones's work
is one of the rarest books relating to Virginia that was
published in the eighteenth century. In 1865, the late
bookseller Sabin, of New York, reprinted a few copies
of it in facsimile, and this reprint has supplied the information that warrants Graham's statement that this
was the first theater erected in North America.

Jones was a fellow of William and Mary College
in Williamsburg, Virginia, afterward a professor of
mathematics in this college, and, as appears from the
title-page of his book, was also chaplain of the House
of Burgesses of Virginia and minister of the Episcopal
church at Jamestown, which was in close proximity
to Williamsburg, the capital.

The work contains a chapter wholly devoted to that
capital, in which, after describing the situation and
plan of the town, William and Mary College, the State
House, the church, which he says "is adorned as the
best church in London," he continues as follows:
"Next there is a large octagon Tower which is the
Magazine or Repository of Arms and Ammunition,
standing far from any house except Jamestown Court
House, for the town is half in Jamestown County and
half in York County. Not far from hence is a large
area for a Market Place, near which is a *Play House*
and good Bowling Green."

The play-house, from the manner in which he refers
to it, was evidently regarded by him as one of the
prominent things of the town, and as such worthy of
being enumerated with the other public structures,

such as the College, the State House, and the Governor's House, which Graham says was then " accounted the most magnificent structure in North America." But there is nothing further respecting the play-house, except the fact that it was in existence in 1722, for Jones had been but two years away from Virginia when he published his book in London in 1724. That nothing more should be found respecting it is not remarkable, for in that early colonial period local occurrences were seldom mentioned in the small-sized journals that existed, for the simple reason that they were generally known to all the inhabitants of the town or place, and were not, therefore, news like intelligence from London or Boston. There was, moreover, no newspaper in Virginia until 1732, when the Virginia " Gazette," which is described as a small dingy sheet with few items of news was published.* In fact, there was not at this time a printing-press in the colony, nor, until many years thereafter, even a bookseller's shop, although there were then in Boston five printing-presses and many booksellers.†

Mr. Edward Eggleston, in an interesting paper, entitled " Social Life in the Colonies," contributed to " The Century Magazine " of July, 1883, says that mention is made of a play on the King's birthday at Williamsburg, in 1718, which I suppose refers to the one mentioned in Governor Spottiswood's letter.

Theodore L. Chasè, in an article in one of the pub-

* Cookes " History of the People of Virginia," Boston, 1890.
† Graham's " History of the United States of North America," Vol. i, p. 145, and note 1 : London, 1836.

lic journals, after calling attention to Jones's work of 1724, "The Present State of Virginia," says that he finds in the Virginia "Gazette" of September 10, 1736, a statement that the young gentlemen of William and Mary College were to enact that evening the tragedy of "Cato," and that therefore, at the hour stated, the comedies of "The Busybody," "The Recruiting Officer," and "The Beaux' Stratagem" were to be enacted by the *company*, from which he infers that the play-house mentioned by Jones was still in existence, and that the "company" who were to enact the comedies mentioned were not, as I understand him, the students of the college, but an organized theatrical company, who were then performing in Williamsburg, where a theater had been built.

It would be out of the ordinary course of things that a play-house like this, close to the market-place, should have been erected for occasional performances by amateurs. A hall in the college would have sufficed for such a purpose, as the halls in old mansions and other structures in England were used for such incidental occasions. It is more probable that it was an ordinary theater, where plays were performed by professional actors.

There are many circumstances that lead to that conclusion. The Virginians were a very different people from the Puritans of New England, and had none of the repugnance to stage plays that prevailed among the latter. They had not, like the Puritans, fled to the wilds of America that they might enjoy unmolested their religious beliefs, and carry out their own ideas of

religion and civil government, but persons who had
gone to Virginia simply to better their condition.   As
Bancroft has described them, they were " a continuation of English society, who were attached to the
monarchy, with a deep reverence for the English
church, and a love for England and English institutions." Upon the overthrow of Charles I., the loyal-
ists in considerable numbers emigrated to Virginia,
many of whom, as the same writer says, brought to the
colony the culture and education that belonged to the
English gentry of that day.

The descendants of these cavalier emigrants were,
at the time to which this inquiry relates,— the early
portion of the eighteenth century,— the dominant
class, politically and socially, in the colony.   They
lived upon large plantations, isolated from each other,
sparsely spread over a wide territory, so that each
plantation might have the advantage of close proximity to water for the transportation of tobacco, which
was the chief product raised by them for export.   In
this respect the province was particularly well adapted
for settlement in this way, as it was traversed not only
by long rivers, but had flowing into their main arteries
innumerable creeks and short streams, which were
navigable for vessels of moderate draught, so that they
had not to leave their plantations to ship or dispose of
their produce, but could load it at the doors of their
own warehouses.*

The facilities which the physical features of the

* Graham, p. 146.

country afforded for easy transportation by water, rendered it unnecessary, as in New England, to settle largely in towns or villages, for the plantations, being large and well peopled, especially after slaves had been introduced from Africa to cultivate them, a plantation had the ordinary facilities of a village or town ; and as the proprietor and his family were not required to labor, there was much intercourse among the planters, with the enjoyment of sports and amusements, for which they had alike the leisure and the disposition. It was a state of things that in time brought about a landed aristocracy, that divided society into two classes, the land-owners or gentry, and their dependants or servants.

It was customary then, especially in London, for men as well as women who had lost reputation to emigrate to Virginia, where, by a life of industry, they might retrieve their character and improve their worldly condition, as a life of industry there brought with it no reproach, which was not the case in London, where, at that time, to labor for subsistence involved the loss of caste. Others were transported thither as a punishment for crime, a class described by Jones as "the poorest, idlest, worst of mankind," but insignificant in number when compared with the shoal of slaves from Africa, by whom the hardest amount of the labor was performed.

Jones, describing the white population of the Colony at this period says: "They were, for the most part, comely, handsome persons, of good features and fine complexions, wearing the best of clothes according to their stations and sometimes beyond their circumstances." He further describes them as "bright and of excellent sense, speaking good English, without any idiom, sharp in trade, conversing with ease upon common subjects, and though of excellent natural capacity diverted by business or inclination from profound study or prying into the depth of things; more inclined to read men by business and conversation than to dive into books; desirous only of learning what was absolutely necessary and in the shortest way; who, through their quick apprehension, had, though it was superficial, a sufficiency of knowledge and fluency of tongue."

He describes the planters generally as "indolent and hospitable, leading easy lives, and not much admiring labor or any manly exercise except horse racing, nor any diversion except cock fighting." Finally, he says: "The habits of life, customs, etc., of the inhabitants were much the same as about London, which they esteem their home, with a contempt for every other part of Great Britain."

After long struggles and many serious trials Virginia was then in a very flourishing condition. "This country," says Jones in the introduction to his book, "has altered wonderfully, and far more advanced and improved in all respects in late years than in the whole century before," and this prosperity was especially felt in Williamsburg, which, though small in respect to resident population, was the only town, for Richmond and Petersburgh were not laid out until 1733, and was the capital of a widely extended province; it was where the Governor resided, where the twelve Councillors or upper house and the House of Burgesses

assembled for legislative purposes, where the Law
Courts were held, and where what might be called the
gentry went, as Jones states, for pleasure.   He says
that " they had balls and assemblies at the Governor's
House, with as fine an entertainment as he had seen
anywhere ; " that the public buildings, the chief of
which was the College, were excelled by few of their
kind in England ; that the stores in the town were
stocked with all sorts of rich goods ; that they had a
number of artificers and convenient ordinaries or inns
for the accommodation of strangers ; that the dwelling-
houses, some of which were of brick, but chiefly of wood,
were large and commodious, lasting and dry, so that
they were warm in winter and cool in summer ; that
the town was laid out in square lots, each one large
enough for a house and garden, so that they had not to
build their houses close together as in other towns,
thus affording a free circulation of air and diminishing
in case of fire the danger of destruction.   Several of
what he calls good families resided permanently in
the capital, and others during what he calls the
" public time."   They live, he says, " in the same neat
manner, dress after the same modes, and behave themselves exactly as the gentry of London ; most families
of any note having their coach, chariot, Berlin or
chaise, and dwelling, as he finally says, " comfortably,
genteelly, pleasantly, and plentifully in this delightful,
healthful, and (I hope) thriving city of Williamsburg."

Cooke, in his " History of the People of Virginia,"
describes Williamsburg at about the middle of the last
century in the winter as the scene of much that was

brilliant and attractive in Virginia society. " It was,"
he says, " the habit of the planters to go there with
their families at this season, to enjoy the pleasures
of the Capital, and one of the highways, Gloucester,
was an animated spectacle of coaches and four, con-
taining the nabobs and their dames; of maidens in silk
and lace, with high healed-shoes and clocked stock-
ings. All these people were engaged in attending the
assemblies at the palace, in dancing at the Appolo, in
snatching the pleasures of the moment and enjoying
life under a régime that seemed mad for enjoyment." . . . The violins seemed to be ever playing
for the diversion of the youths and maidens; cocks
were fighting, horsemen riding, students mingled in
the throng in their academic dress, and his Serene
Excellency went to open the House of Burgesses in
his coach, drawn by six milk-white horses. It was a
scene full of gaiety and abandon, and Williamsburg
was never more brilliant than at this period.*

I have been thus particular in describing the place
and its inhabitants to show that it was just the kind
of capital that had alike the taste and the means to
erect and support a theater, if not regularly, at least
for a certain period of the year, or what, in theatrical
parlance, is called a " season." Although, according
to another writer, it had only about eighty houses and
consequently but a small resident population, there
must have been a considerable influx of visitors for
business or pleasure, and this is the class upon which

* Part III, ch. 6.

a theater is chiefly dependent for support. Mr. Gaisford, in his historical sketch of "The Drama in New Orleans," after remarking that perhaps in no city of the world of such a limited population were there so many edifices for dramatic purposes as in New Orleans, — not temporary structures, but for the most part solid, substantial buildings,— accounts for this circumstance by the fact that in the winter months the Crescent City was a great rendezvous for strangers, young men attracted there by the prospect of commercial employment; skilful mechanics who were largely remunerated; and an immense number of transient persons with ample means and good incomes who, being without acquaintances or at least without friends, could not enjoy themselves in so rational a manner as in a well conducted theater, who, he says, "could always be relied upon and were the main support of such establishments." * Something of this kind would then, necessarily, exist in Williamsburg, as the social, political, and business center of Virginia. The people had, as Jones remarks, the habits and tastes of the British metropolis, and in London, at that time, no taste was more general or widely diffused than a taste for the drama. Some of the most renowned of English players were then upon the stage, such as Colley Cibber, Wilks, Barton Booth, Johnson, Bullock, Quin, Macklin, Mrs. Porter, and Mrs. Oldfield, and Betterton; Doggett, Mrs. Barry, and Mrs. Bracegirdle had but recently left it.

* "The Drama in New Orleans," by John Gaisford, etc., pp. 7, 8. New Orleans, 1849.

The licentiousness that had prevailed alike in the composition and representation of plays was rapidly passing away and a better class of persons went to the theater. Addison, writing at this period, says: "I cannot be of the opinion of the reformers of manners in their severity toward plays; but must allow that a good play, acted before a well-bred audience, must raise very proper incitement to good behaviour, and be the most quick and the most prevailing method of giving young people a turn of sense and breeding.

"When," he continues, "the character drawn by a judicious poet is presented by the person, the manner, the look, and the motion of an accomplished player, what may not be brought to pass by seeing generous things performed before our eyes? The stage is the best mirror of human life; let me therefore recommend the oft use of a theatre as the most agreeable and easy method of making a polite and moral gentry, which would end in rendering the rest of the people regular in their behaviour and ambitious of laudable undertakings." *

The stage was then approximating to what Addison would have it. In the reign of Queen Anne an act was passed forbidding anything to be represented upon it that was derogatory to religion under the penalty of being deprived of the right to act, and at no period, before or since, did the stage exercise so much influence over all classes of society in London. It was the standard or model for dress and manners,

* Davies, "Dramatic Miscellanies," Vol. iii, ch. 17.

for dress and manners were matters of much more importance socially then than they are now; and these social habits and tastes were transported across the Atlantic, at least to Virginia, as appears from the account which Jones gives of the people of Williamsburg, and we know from other sources that among the better classes, not only in Virginia but in many of the other colonies, great attention was paid to dress, to the cultivation of manners, and to the art of conversation.

A comparatively small expenditure was all that was necessary for erecting a suitable theater, or converting a warehouse or other building into one. Theaters in English towns were then, as they are at the present day in the small towns in Germany, humble and inexpensive structures. The compensation of actors, save in exceptionable instances, was then very small. It supplied little more than a subsistence, and even that was precarious. It was small even in London. Betterton, who has been called the greatest actor, except Garrick, the English stage has ever known,—who, Colley Cibber says, " was, as an actor, what Shakespeare was as an author, without a competitor," —never received more than four pounds a week, and though a man of economical habits and exemplary life, died, after a career upon the stage of half a century, in limited circumstances. Yet, notwithstanding the smallness of their pecuniary reward, players were never wanting; the stage has such a fascination for those who have an aptitude for it and occasionally for those who have but little, that a life of laborious diligence and pecuniary struggle is willingly undergone for the nightly pleasure of appearing before the footlights and sharing in the mimic scene.

It may not unreasonably be supposed, then, that at an early period members of this ill-requited profession made their way to Virginia, like others with whom the world had gone hard, and found among a people of London habits and London tastes sufficient inducement to get a company together, and open a theater in a capital that then contained the most aristocratic and cultivated society in the colonies.

I stated in the paper here reprinted that it appeared by an advertisement in Bradford's "Gazette," in 1733, that a play-house existed in New York in that year, and that this reference was all that I had found respecting it. Some years afterward Mr. T. F. De Voe, to whom I have before referred, and who is more generally known as the author of the "Market Book," informed me by letter that he had found in the "New England and Boston Gazette" of January 1, 1733, under the head of New York News of December 11, 1732, the following account of the opening of this theater in 1732.

"On the 6th instant, the *New Theatre* in the building of the Hon. Rip Van Dam, Esq., was opened with the comedy of the *Recruiting Officer*, the part of Worthy acted by the ingenious Mr. Thos. Heady, Barber and Peruque maker to his Honor."

That it is referred to in this paragraph as the New Theater would seem to imply that there had been a previous one, or some building or place where dramatic performances were given. Governor Burnet, who had been the governor of the Colony from 1720 to 1728, was a highly cultivated man. He is described by Smith, the first historian of New York, as "a man of sense and of polite breeding, a well-read scholar, sprightly, and of a social disposition. Being devoted to his books, he abstained from all those excesses into which his pleasurable relish would have otherwise plunged him. He studied the art of recommending himself to the people, had nothing of the moroseness of a scholar, was gay and condescending, affected no pomp, visited every family of reputation, and often diverted himself in open converse with the ladies, by whom he was very much admired;" to which he adds that he was very fond of New York, his marriage there having connected him with a numerous family besides an unusual acquaintance, and that he left it with reluctance.* By such a man the drama might be looked upon as favorably as it was at that period by Addison, and it may be that during the eight years of his administration dramatic performances were given in the city, which was the capital of the province. Rip Van Dam, who was the owner of the building in which the New Theater was opened, was the acting governor from the time of Burnet's departure until the arrival of Governor Cosby in 1732, a few months before the New Theater was opened, and was obviously the personage denominated "his honor," to whom "the ingenious Mr. Thomas Heady," who acted the part of Worthy,

---

* Smith's "History of New York" with a continuation, pp. 239, 240, 271 : Albany, 1814.

stood in the important relation, in his own eyes, of barber and peruque maker.

The New Theater, as stated in the advertisement, was in the building belonging to Rip Van Dam, and as Kean & Murray's Company, who came to New York eighteen months afterward,— that is, in February, 1750,— hired, as stated in my former paper, "a large room in the building on Nassau street, belonging to the estate of Rip Van Dam, the two theaters, that of 1732 and 1750, were probably in the same building, now generally referred to as the Nassau Street Theater.

The comedy with which the New Theater was opened in 1732, "The Recruiting Officer," is the earliest play known to have been acted in North America, for though, as has been stated, there was a play-house in Williamsburg ten years before, it is not known what plays were acted there until 1736, when four are referred to, and "The Recruiting Officer" was one of them, which had the attraction for Virginia that the Colony was referred to in it. It was a popular play in the early part of the last century, and continued to be acted frequently for nearly a century and a half. Much of its wit and sprightliness is in language that would not be tolerated now on any stage, as also some of the minor incidents of the plot; but its raciness in this respect was no doubt, at that time, a part of its attraction, and then its leading parts have been enacted by great players. It was written by George Farquhar, one of four dramatists — Wycherley, Congreve, Vanbrugh, and himself — who are generally referred to as the leading comic dramatists of the Restoration; and of

the four, this production of Farquhar was the one
that continued the longest upon the stage. Leigh
Hunt, a very competent critic, considered "The Recruiting Officer" one of the very best of Farquhar's
plays. Every character, he says, of any importance,
is a genuine transcript from nature; that there is a
charm of gaiety and good humor throughout it, and
the fresh, clear air of a ruddy-making remote English town neighborhooded by ample elegance. It was
performed in New York in 1843, and was revived February 8, 1885, in the same city, by Mr. Augustin Daly,
who has done so much to enable the present generation to see what these witty and sprightly old comedies are when represented on the stage, so far as it can
be done, by detaching from them what would be objectionable in the present age, and which, in the revival
of "The Recruiting Officer," he did by reducing its five
acts to three. It will not, I think, be out of place to
show what was the result by inserting two clever criti-
cisms that appeared in two of the New York journals
on the morning after this revival, by writers who were
not only excellent dramatic critics, but also evidently
thoroughly well acquainted with the dramatic literature
of the period when "The Recruiting Officer" was written, and the correctness of whose account of the performance on that evening I am able to corroborate,
having been myself one of the audience on that
occasion. There is a freshness and vividness moreover in an account of the performance of a play written immediately after seeing it, which can rarely be
imparted afterwards.

This is one of the articles:

"THE RECRUITING OFFICER.

Captain Plume	Mr. DREW
Captain Brazen	Mr. PARKES
Justice Balance	Mr. FISHER
Sergeant Kite	Mr. LEWIS
Mr. Worthy	Mr. SKINNER
Bullock	Mr. GILBERT
Appletree	Mr. BOND
Pearman	Mr. WILKS
Balance's Steward	Mr. BEEKMAN
Mistress Melinda	Miss VIRGINIA DREHER
Rose	Miss May FIELDING
Lucy	Miss MAY IRWIN
Sylvia	Miss ADA REHAN

" I am called Captain, sir, by all the drawers and groom-porters in London," said Miss Ada Rehan at Daly's Theater last night. And bravely she wore her red coat and sword, the martial twist in her cravat, the fierce knot in her periwig, the cane upon her button, and the dice in her pocket. The audience were in ecstasies.

It was a revival of " The Recruiting Officer," by George Farquhar. The manners of Queen Anne's day were reproduced on Mr. Daly's stage. *Captain Plume* and *Sergeant Kite* were enlisting the country lads and paying court to the country lasses. *Justice Balance* was keeping watch over the morals of his daughter *Sylvia*. Sprightly *Mistress Melinda* was intriguing for the hand of young *Worthy*. *Brazen* was bragging of his service in Flanders against the French and in Hungary against the Turks. The atmosphere was charged with love, and the stage resounded with the tap of the drum.

The audience was in a curious and observant mood. The doings on the stage were of a wholly unfamiliar kind. The language sounded strangely fantastic to modern ears. Ladies held their breath at the bygone sentiment of the play. Men met in groups between the acts and wondered what was the secret of its original success. Its secret was tolerably simple. It was written at the time of Marlborough's earlier victories. Blenheim had just been won. A military fever possessed the country. Rustics went marching round the fields with ribbons in their caps. The recruiting officer was seen in every town. The popular song of the hour was:

> Over the hills and over the main
> To Flanders, Portugal and Spain:
> The Queen commands and we'll obey;
> Over the hills and far away.

Moreover, there was a steady flow of indecency in the comedy. The town had been growing dull. Congreve had retired into the intimacy of the Duchess of Marlborough. Wycherley was writing feeble poems under the tutorship of that rising young man, Alexander Pope. Vanbrugh was giving his attention to architecture. Jeremy Collier and his moral tractate had exorcised the merry devils off the stage, and the pit mourned their departure. So "The Recruiting Officer," with its broad jests, was particularly welcome. *Captain Plume*, with his amorous devices, became the ideal of the army, and pretty *Rose*, with her chickens, furnished laughter for the mess-room and coffee-houses.

Human nature has not much changed. Mr. Daly's audience last night was as fashionable an audience as could be gathered in the city. Yet the few suggestive lines which he has left in the piece excited the loudest laugh. Americans are not squeamish with these old plays. They know that the comedies of the Restoration were not models of propriety. They know that George Farquhar, the rollicking Irish captain, was not a preacher of morality. And if the piece hung fire at times, if it seemed a trifle heavy and monotonous, it was because the spectators had been credited with a prudery which they did not seem to possess.

The company was a little out of its element. Mr. Drew, in particular, should have been livelier and airier, conducting his love affairs with as light a touch as Charles Mathews might have conducted them in other days, or Mr. Wallack to-day. Mr. Fisher, too, pressed with too heavy a hand on such niceties of character as have been discovered in *Justice Balance ;* and Mr. James Lewis, though discreet and refined in his humor, extracted none of the exuberant fun from *Sergeant Kite* with which critics of the past have supposed that unscrupulous personage to overflow. Mr. Skinner was a dignified young lover, and Mr. Parkes amused as *Brazen*. But the honors of the evening rested with Miss Virginia Dreher, who looked radiantly beautiful in a web of lace and gold, and with Miss Ada Rehan, who had the bold step, the rakish toss and the impudent air of your true military gallant. She was not Peg Woffington, perhaps, but she was a charming woman in disguise, and the town will be curious to see her.

This is the other :

"THE RECRUITING OFFICER."

Another " first night " in Mr. Daly's comfortable theater, and the same assemblage of well-dressed people, with faces one knows by sight on every side, and pleasurable expectancy the predominating sensation. " Love on Crutches " has ambled gracefully out of sight, and instead of the fresh daintiness of the modern play there were to come rollicking humor, the buoyant spirits, the intrigue and broad wit of old English comedy. No longer the New York fine lady, Miss Rehan was to depict the healthy English maiden of nearly two centuries ago, and to masquerade as well in the character of *Jack Wilful;* Mr. Drew, who had so cleverly portrayed the young New Yorker of the last quarter of the nineteenth century, was to assume the becoming uniform, the rakish air, and the frolicsome manners of a British officer in the first quarter of the eighteenth; instead of a meek and virtuous family physician, Mr. Lewis was to be seen as a rattling and reprehensible recruiting sergeant. In other words, George Farquhar's bright and witty comedy, " The Recruiting Officer," was to be revealed to a generation of playgoers who scarcely remembered even its title, so long had it been left upon the shelf. Pleasurable expectations of the production were in many respects realized. The comedy was tastefully mounted, though without extravagance, the costumes were handsome and appropriate to the time represented, and consequently the stage pictures revealed were both handsome and quaint. That the old-time flavor was fully preserved in the action it would be folly to say. An intelligent performance of Farquhar's comedy was given, however, with much of the original text, and everybody present interested in the history and literature of the English stage found abundant entertainment. Mr. Daly has compressed the five acts of Farquhar into three, slightly altering the sequence of some of the scenes, expunging lines of dubious meaning, and many not at all dubious, and quickening the dénouement. While " The Recruiting Officer," is not so ingeniously constructed as " The Beaux' Stratagem," its dialogue bristles with repartee, every character is clearly defined, and the plot is clever though slight. The scene is laid at Shrewsbury, and the personages are simple townsfolk and military men. There is a quartet of lovers, a wise father, a noisy braggart, the *Sergeant,* who fills the position of intriguing valet to the hero, a designing lady's maid, a knowing market girl, and a trio of bumpkins. The heroine, being sent away by her father to avoid her lover, returns in male attire to test the hero's affections, and after some strange experiences weds him. The play, of course, has famous associations. Peg Woffington played *Sylvia* when the veteran Quin was *Justice Balance ;* Elliston played *Captain Plume,* and in later years this was one of Charles Kemble's favorite parts ; Munden and Knight were the original representatives of the two recruits, *Pearmain* and *Appletree,** and Irish Johnstone was *Sergeant Kite.* In that cast Ann Oldfield was *Sylvia,* Cibber *Brazen,* and Wilks, Farquhar's nearest friend, *Captain Plume.* It was a fancy of Farquhar's friends that *Plume* was a portrait of himself. He had been a dashing officer during his brief and eventful career, as well as actor and dramatist. Farquhar's life was a sad one, in spite of the legacy of merriment he left to the world in his works. He left college to go upon the stage, which, after accidentally wounding a brother actor in a fencing combat, he abandoned for the army. He died at the age of thirty, leaving no fortune for his family, although within a decade he had written seven successful comedies, " Love and a Bottle," " The Constant Couple," " The Inconstant ; or, Wine Works Wonders," " The Stage Coach," " The Recruiting Officer," and " The Beaux' Stratagem," during the run of which he expired, in the Spring of 1707. Farquhar was a man of genius, a keen observer, and, like most of his kind, a stanch foe to all pretense. His low-comedy characters were true to nature in their conceits and frailties, as well as in their manner of speech ; his high-bred dames were not always circumspect in their behavior, while his young gentlemen were devil-may-care fellows, glib of tongue, affable, generous, but not exactly proper. He belonged to his

* This is an error in the writer, they were Norris and Fairbank, and the original *Sergeant Kite* was Estcourt.

age, and, compared with the work of some of his contemporaries and immediate predecessors, his writings were purity itself. With the exception of "The Inconstant" we do not remember that any of his comedies had been performed here in recent years, until "The Recruiting Officer" was seen last evening. They demand of actors dashing manners, freedom and breadth of style, which few performers of the present day possess. The charm of last evening's representation lay in the portrayal of *Sylvia* by Miss Rehan. Indeed this was the only individual piece of work that could be said to have any charm, and although *Sylvia* is the heroine the part is scarcely more important than at least two of the others. Miss Rehan was not only successful in catching the spirit of the piece, and transmitting it to the audience, so far as her own part was concerned, but she invested the character with womanly tenderness and delicacy, and put more meaning into a few important lines of the text than appears on the surface. As *Sylvia* herself, she was the affectionate and dutiful daughter, who felt more sorrow for her brother's death, doubtless, than the author intended; as *Master Jack Wilful*, and his *alter ego*, *Captain Pinch*, who took snuff with a pinch, and in short, could do anything at a pinch, her imitation of the foppish manners and languid nonchalance of the London buck was deliciously droll and seemed not a bit incongruous, though it is not likely that it was so pronounced as Mistress Ann Oldfield's treatment of the same passages. Miss Rehan, in short, was thoroughly at home in the old comedy. If her work was not strictly in keeping with traditions, it was still delightful and artistic. She interpreted Farquhar in her own way, but without missing his meaning, except where his meaning would not be tasteful to a modern audience. Her treatment of the scenes with *Rose*, for instance, was admirable; and the tact and refinement of the actress were needed in these in spite of careful "editing" and expunging. It is needless to say that Miss Rehan presented a handsome picture in the fine raiment of *Master Wilful*, and the well-setting uniform of the gay *Captain*. Mr. Charles Fisher handled the character of old *Balance* in his accustomed manner; the mode of old comedy is familiar to this veteran, for he was educated to it, and was a rising actor when Farquhar's comedy was last given at the old "Park," forty-two years ago. Miss Dreher spoke the lines of languid *Miss Melinda* in the right spirit, and was a fine lady to the life, but the part is of little interest. Mr. Drew bore himself well in his uniform, and his acting was extremely good at some points, notably, in the combat with *Brazen*. But he lacks the joyous, rattling style essential to the proper rendering of such a character. No one, for instance, would ever take *Captain Plume*, as played by Mr. Drew, for a portrait of George Farquhar. Mr. Lewis, as *Kite*, was Mr. Lewis; Mr. Skinner, as *Worthy*, was Guy Roverly dressed for a masquerade; *Brazen*, in the hands of Mr. Parkes, should be renamed Wooden; *Bullock* was made by Mr. Gilbert, an ill-fed fellow, dry instead of unctuous, and the two recruits were colorless sketches. Miss Fielding was pretty and interesting as the chicken girl, and Miss Irwin amusing as *Melinda's* maid. At times the performance dragged when Miss Rehan was off the stage, but Mr. Daly is to be thanked for the revival all the same, which, as we have intimated, is well worth seeing.

Which ends this second writer's notice of the revival.

The first representation of the play was at Drury Lane in 1706. The original Sylvia was Mrs. Oldfield, a tall, beautiful, finely formed woman, with an exquisite, clear, and powerful voice, that made her as impressive in tragedy as she was fascinating in comedy. Fielding, the novelist, says that her "ravishing perfection made her the admiration of every eye and every ear"; and Colley Cibber and other contemporaries unite in giving her the most unstihted praise. Such an actress, in such a part as Sylvia, the most interesting character in the play, must have been very attractive, especially in that portion of it where Sylvia appears in male attire, dressed as a young officer. It was to her that Pope referred, according to Warton, in the well-known lines, descriptive of a feminine wish at the closing moment of life :

> " Odious ! in woollen ! 'twould a saint provoke "
> (Were the last words that poor Narcissa spoke).
> " No, let a charming chintz and Brussels lace
> Wrap my cold limbs and shade my lifeless face.
> One would not, sure, be frightful when one's dead
> And — Betty — give this cheek a little Red."

The original Captain Plume, the recruiting officer, was Wilks, the most distinguished actor at that time on the English stage, and this part continued for a long time thereafter to be a favorite one with actors who had the advantages of a handsome face, a fine person, and the temperament to impart to it that vivacity and airiness that the character requires. The original Kite, the recruiting sergeant, a part that affords great scope for the powers of a low comedian, was Estcourt, a famous mimic, of whom Colley Cibber says: " This man was so amazing and extraordinary a mimic that

no man or woman from the coquette to the privy
councillor ever moved or spoke before him but he
could carry their voice, look, mien, and motion in-
stantly into another company," and he adds, " even to
the manner of thinking of an eminent pleader of the
bar with every, the least article and singularity of his
utterance so perfectly imitated that he was the very
alter ipse, scarcely to be distinguished from his original." [1]   Farquhar, the author of the comedy, schooled
him for this particular part, his performance of which
has been highly praised.   "Witness" says Dowse, "his
Sergeant Kite; he is not only excellent in it, but a
superlative mimic."   "Mr. Estcourt," says Chet-
wood, "the original Sergeant Kite, every night of
performance entertained the audience with a variety
of little catches and flights of humor that pleased all
but his critics."

This allusion to his critics refers to Cibber and some
others who, whilst admitting his great powers as a
mimic, declared that he was but an indifferent actor,
an opinion in which others who were equally competent to judge did not concur, and which on Cibber's
part was attributed to his desire to play leading parts,
to which he could not succeed during Estcourt's life.
Estcourt may by his imitations of their acting or pecu-
liarities have offended actors and others, who, however much they might enjoy such a representation of
others, may have looked very differently upon a like
representation of themselves, a good illustration of

[1] Life of Cibber, by Bell, Chambers ed., 105, 106.

which is found in an anecdote of Estcourt and Sir
Godfrey Kneller, the celebrated portrait painter of
that period.

Secretary Craggs, when a young man, in company
with some of his friends, went with Estcourt to Sir Godfrey Kneller's, and whispered to him that a gentleman
present was able to give such a representation of many
among his most principal patrons as would occasion
the greatest surprise.   Estcourt accordingly, at the
artist's earnest desire, mimicked Lords Somers, Hali-
fax, Godolphin, and others so exactly that Kneller
was delighted and laughed heartily at the imitation.
Craggs gave a signal as previously concerted, and
Estcourt immediately imitated Kneller himself, who
cried out in a transport of ungovernable conviction,
" Nay, there you are out, man.   By G——, that 's not
me ! "

In the colonial society, or " people of figure," as they
were then called in New York, where so much de-
pended upon manners, well-arranged apparel and a
flowing wig, a peruke maker was, at least in his own
estimation, a person of consequence, as appears from
the manner in which Mr. Heady is referred to in the
paragraph that has been quoted, and also from an
announcement that appeared in the " New York
Weekly Post Boy " of March 5, 1750, about three
weeks after the opening of the Nassau Street Theater
by Kean & Murray's company, as mentioned in my
former paper, which announcement is as follows :

" This is to acquaint the public that there is
lately arrived from London the *Wonder* of the *World*,

an honest Barber and Peruke Maker, who might have worked for the King if his Majesty would have employed him; it was not for the want of money that he· came here, for he had enough of that at Home; nor for the want of Business that he advertises himself; but to acquaint the gentlemen and ladies that such a *Person is now in Town* living near *Rosemary Lane*, where Gentlemen and Ladies may be supplied with Goods as follows, viz.: Tyes, Full Bottoms, Myers, Spencers, Fox-Tails, Ramilies, Tucks, Cut kinds of head coverings and adornments, and bob Perukes; also Ladies' Talemalongues and Towers, after the Manner that is now wore at Court. By their humble and obedient Servant,

"JOHN STILL."

The hibernicism that he did not put in the advertisement for the want of business, nor to make money, of which he had plenty, but merely to apprise the ladies and gentlemen that *such a person* was then in town, was, if genuine, an exhibition of enormous self-importance, or it was what is more probable, a comic effort to attract attention to his calling by one who was something of an adept in that way, who may have been a member of the theatrical company that were then performing, and who followed the three pursuits of a barber, a peruke maker, and an actor.

It would appear that there was a second opening of a theater in New York seven years afterwards. All that I know respecting it is that there is a manuscript volume in the possession of Mr. William Nelson, of

Paterson, New Jersey, handsomely engrossed with ornamental lettering, entitled:

POEMS
ON
SEVERAL OCCASIONS
BY
ARCHIBALD HOME, ESQ.,
Late Secretary and One of His Majesties Council
for the province of New Jersey North America,

which was purchased by Mr. Nelson from a London dealer in 1890, and that one of these poems is entitled

PROLOGUE,

INTENDED FOR THE SECOND OPENING OF THE
THEATRE AT NEW YORK, ANNO 1739,

which is as follows:

> Encourag'd by th' Indulgence you have shown,
> Again we strive to entertain the Town,
>   This gen'rous Town which nurs'd our infant Stage
>   And cast a Shelter o'er its tender Age,
> It's young Attempts beyond their Merits prais'd
> Fond of the little Bantling she had rais'd
>   Go on to cherish to a Stronger Size
>   This Spur to Virtue, this keen Scourge to Vice!
> Ye Faultless Fair, lend all your influence here!
> O Patronize the Child, you cannot Fear.

> Oft when the Serious Admonition Fails
> O'er the lov'd Fault the Comick Mask prevails;
>   Safe From the Bar, the Pulpit, and the Throne,
>   Vice blushing yields to ridicule alone.

This ancient Greece this the Great Romans knew,
They held th' instructive Mirrour Fair to view;
   That each his own Deformities might trace
   And smooth his features by the Faithful Glass.

   When Arts and Sciences began to Smile,
And shed their Lustre on our Parent Isle,
   Attendant on their Steps the Drama came,
   Like theirs th' Improvement of Mankind her Aim;
Intent on this with them she journeys West,
To our New World, a wish'd, a welcome Guest;
   Here pleas'd she sees her Stage erect its head,
   Her Children honour'd, & her Servants Fed;
Prophetick views in you her second Rome
And swells her Breast with Empire yet to come.*

The researches of the writer of an article in "The New-York Times" of December the 15th, 1895, has brought to light some information hitherto unknown of these early. American theaters. He has examined the newspaper files of the Library Society in Charles-

---

*A MS. volume, small 4°, Pp. (xvii), I–CXXX; Appendix, pp. XVI. Handsomely engrossed, with ornamental or fancy lettering for the title, the whole apparently the work of a professional clerk. Bound in old mottled calf, with gilt border, stamped back once gilt and lettered.

POEMS

By

A. H.

ESQR

MS.

Bought from a London dealer in 1890, by William Nelson, of Paterson, New Jersey.

ton, South Carolina, from 1732, and finds, on the 24th
of January, 1735, that a play was acted in Charles
Town, as the name was then written, and he gives this
advertisement of it in the "South Carolina Gazette,"
dated, as was then customary, from Jan. 18, 1734–35:

On Friday, the 24th inst., in the Court Room, will be attempted a tradgedy called "The Orphan, or The Unhappy
Marriage."

Tickets will be delivered out on Tuesday next, at Mr. Shepheard's, at 40s. each.

Forty shillings would seem to be a high price at that
time to pay for a ticket to a dramatic entertainment.
But what the value of a shilling was then in South
Carolina compared to the value of a pound sterling, I
do not know. The price of a box ticket at Kean &
Murray's theater in Nassau street fifteen years afterwards was five shillings New York currency, which
was about the value of two dollars at the present day,
and if the value of the South Carolina currency at
that day was anything near that of New York, this
high price for admission would imply either that the
Court House where the performance of Otway's Orphan
took place did not afford room for many spectators or
that the number of persons who were expected to pa-
tronize the entertainment was small, so that a high price
of admission was necessary to meet the expenses and
afford some remuneration to the players, who, I infer,
were a regular theatrical company, as a charge was
made for admission, and the performances were continued once a week, from the 24th of January to March

23, 1735-36, during which tragedies, comedies, farces, and other entertainments were given.

The writer in the "Times" says that the play announced in the advertisement, Otway's "Orphan," was performed, though the next "Gazette" took no notice of it, the "local" being of the briefest character; but the number of the "Gazette" of February, 1736, published the Prologue spoken on the opening night, which has at least the merit of easy versification and of being appropriate to such an occasion: He gives it as follows:

PROLOGUE.

When first Columbus touch'd this distant shore,
And vainly hoped his Fears and Dangers o'er,
One boundless Wilderness in view appear'd
No Champain Plains or rising Cities cheer'd
His wearied Eye.
Monsters unknown travers'd the hideous Waste,
And men more savage than the Beasts they chased.
But mark! How soon these gloomy Prospects clear,
And the new World's late Horrors disappear.
The Soil obedient to the industrious swains,
What happy Harvests crown their honest Pains,
And Peace and Plenty triumph o'er the Plains.
What various products float on every Tide?
What numerous Navies in our Harbors ride?
Tillage and Trade conjoin their friendly Aid,
T' enrich, the thriving Boy and lovely Maid,
Hispania, 'tis true, her precious mines engross'd,
And bore her shining Entrails to its Coast.
Britannia more humane supplies her wants,
The British sense and British beauty plants.

> The aged Sire beholds with sweet surprise
> In foreign climes a numerous offspring rise,
> Sense, Virtue, Worth, and Honour stand confest
> In each brave male, his prosperous hands have blessed,
> While the admiring Eye improved may trace,
> The Mother's Charms in each chaste Virgin's Face.
> Hence we presume to usher in those Arts
> Which oft have warm'd the best and bravest Hearts.
> Faint our Endeavours, wide are our Essays,
> We strive to please, but can't pretend to Praise;
> Forgiving Smiles o'er pay the grateful task,
> Those all we hope and all we humbly ask.

The further information that this interesting article contains it will be more satisfactory to give in the author's own words:

" The Orphan " was repeated January 28, and again February 4, with the addition of " a new Pantomime Entertainment in Grotesque Characters, called, ' The Adventures of Harlequin and Scaramouch, with the Burgo-Master Trick'd.' "

After this run of three nights it was necessary to change the programme, and so the " Gazette " for February 18, 1734–35, announces " ' The Opera of Flora; or, Hob in the Well,' with the Dance of the two Pierrots and a new Pantomime Entertainment, etc., to begin at 6 o'clock precisely."

On Tuesday, March 25, they played the comedy called " The Spanish Fryar; or, The Double Discovery," and on Thursday of the same week the play was repeated " for the benefit of Monimia." Who was Monimia?

This benefit seems to have closed the season, but
the people must have been pleased, for on May 3 the
following advertisement appears :

Any gentlemen that are disposed to encourage the exhibition
of plays next Winter, may have the sight of the proposals for a
subscription at Mr. Shepheard's in Broad Street.   And any persons that are desirous of having a share in the performance
thereof, upon application to Mr. Shepheard shall receive a satisfactory answer.   N. B.—The subscription will be closed the last
day of this month.

There is not another word in " The Gazette " con-
cerning theatrical affairs until January 24, 1735–36,
when the proposals appear to have borne fruit, for it is
announced that —

On Thursday, the 12th of February, will be opened the new
theatre in Dock Street, in which will be performed the comedy
called " The Recruiting Officer."

Tickets for the pitt and boxes will be delivered at Mr. Charles
Shepheard's, on Thursday, the 5th of February. Boxes, 30s ; pitt,
20s ; and tickets for the gallery, 15s, which will be delivered at the
theatre the day of playing.

N. B.— The doors will be opened all the afternoon.   The sub-
scribers are desired to send to the stage door in the forenoon to
bespeak places, otherwise it will be too late.

Dunlap evidently had never heard of the " new
theatre in Dock Street," for he says that " in 1773 the
first theater was built in Charleston, S. C., David
Douglass having gained permission from the magistrates, and being invited by the inhabitants.   In September he went thither and the company followed him.
They played fifty-one nights in that city, closing the

campaign in June, 1774. On October 24, 1774, the first Congress agreed to discountenance gaming, cock fighting, exhibition of shows, plays, and other expensive diversions and entertainments."

The Charles Town " Gazette " does not notice so important an event as the opening of the first theater in the South, and probably on this continent, in its news columns, but the advertisements announce that on February 23 Otway's " Orphan " was played, and the next " Gazette " announces:

By desire of the officers of the Troop and Foot Companies, at the new theatre, Queen street, will be acted on Tuesday next, a comedy called the " Recruiting Officer," with several entertainments as will be expressed in the great bills.

Tickets to be had at Mr. Charles Shepheard's and at the theatre.

Charles Town was at that time a rapidly growing town, and plebeian " Dock " street, as shown by the advertisements, had been changed to " Queen " street, as it is still known.

Once a week seems to have been the rule for the plays, but the next piece, George Lillo's famous " The London Merchant, or the History of George Barnwell," was not put upon the boards until March 9. Seven days later it was repeated " for the last time," with the addition of a farce, " The Devil to Pay, or the Wives Metamorphosed." This was Coffey's celebrated work, whose " female character Nell * * * made the fortunes of several actresses."

The season seems to have closed with the perennial

"Orphan" and the above-named farce, which were
played March 23, 1735–36. This is all that can be
gleaned from the "Gazette" as to the plays and
theater, but the new venture seems to have very soon
come to grief. The "Gazette" for May 22–29 contains this epigram :

ON THE SALE OF THE THEATRE.

How cruel Fortune, and how fickle, too,
To crop the Method made for making you!
Changes tho' common, yet when great they prove,
Make men distrust the care of Mighty Jove;
Half made in thought (though not in fact) we find
You bought and sold, but left poor H. behind.
P. S.—Since so it is ne'er mind the silly trick,
The pair will please, when Pierrot makes you sick.

Who sold and who bought is a mystery, but the
transaction did not change the theater to other uses,
for the "Gazette" announces: "A ball at the play-
house in Queen street on February 3 next. To begin
at 6 o'clock." In the paper for January 8–15, 1737,
and in May of the same year: "At the request of the
Ancient and Honorable Society of Free and Accepted
Masons, at the theatre in Queen Street, on Thursday
next, the 26th instant, will be performed a comedy,
called 'The Recruiting Officer,' with a prologue, epilogue and song suitable to the occasion, to which will
be added a new dance called 'Harlequin,' and the
clown and the song, 'Mad Tom' in proper habili-
ments, by a person that has never yet appeared upon
the stage."

This performance seems to have been a great success, for the next " Gazette " accords it this most extended notice :

CHARLESTOWN, May 28.

On Thursday night last " The Recruiting Officer " was acted for the entertainment of the ancient and honorable society of Free and Accepted Masons, who came to the Play House about 7 o'clock, in the usual manner, and made a very decent and solemn appearance; there was a fuller house on this occasion than ever had been known in this place, and the entered apprentice and masters songs, sung upon the stage, which were joined in chorus by the Masons in the pitt to the satisfaction and entertainment of the whole audience.

After the play the Masons returned to the lodge at Mr. Shepheard's, in the same order observed in coming to the Play House.

Mad Tom's song must have been taken from " King Lear," and, if so, is the first recorded instance of the production of any of Shakespeare's works on this continent.

The most careful search has failed to find any mention of plays for some years, but a map of Charlestown dated 1738 marks the site of the theater on the south side of Queen, a little west of Church street, on the lot of land now occupied by the rear portion of the old Planters' Hotel, within less than a hundred yards of the Huguenot and St. Philip's Churches, and in October, 1743, a ball is advertised to take place at the theater in Queen street.

A similar notice appears in the paper for November 19, 1774, and the next link is an advertisement in the " Gazette," October 3, 1748, of a school " over against the Play House," and the following extract from

" an exhortation to the inhabitants of South Carolina,"
written by a Quakeress, Sophia Hume, in 1748, and
published in London in 1752.

The good lady, after setting forth the sins of the
people of the province, says : " You have no masquer-
ades nor music gardens to entertain you, neither are
theatrical entertainments frequent among you," which
implies that they took place sometimes.

May her shade grant pardon for the use of her book
in an article on the play-house.

But Sophia Hume exhorted in vain, for the " Gazette," in its issue for October 3, 1754, contains this
rather contradictory advertisement :

" At the New Theatre on Monday next, (by a company of comedians from London,) a tragedy called the
' Fair Penitent.' Tickets to be had of Mr. John
Remington and at the printer's.   Price, stage box 50s.;
front and side boxes, 40s. ; pitt, 30s., and gallery, 20s."

The " Gazette " dramatic reporter says of the play :
" Last Monday evening the New Theatre in this town
was opened, when a company of comedians performed
the tragedy called the ' Fair Penitent,' much to the
satisfaction of the audience."

The theatrical history of Charleston from this time
on, however, is familiar.*

In the paucity of information about the drama in
America at this early period, it may be admissible to
refer to what fiction has attempted respecting it in a
novel by John Esten Cooke, entitled " The Virginia

* " New-York Times," Sunday, December 15, 1895.

Comedians," in which he describes the Williamsburg
theater, and the representation in it of a play of Shakespeare's.   As Shakespeare expressed it, "imagination
bodies forth the form of things unknown," and men of
genius, like Sir Walter Scott and the elder Dumas, could,
in the exercise of this faculty, represent scenes and incidents of the past more vividly and apparently as truth-
fully as can be derived from the scant material usually
left for the historian — an illustration of which will be
found in Dumas's account of the trial and execution
of Charles I., in his sequel to "The Three Musketeers,"
" Twenty Years After"; and in Scott's novels there
are many like illustrations.   "This history," says Fielding, in the preface to his celebrated novel which he calls
" The History of Tom Jones," " differs from other histories in this, that in other histories nothing is true but
the names, whilst in this everything is true but the
names"; and the author of " The Virginia Comedians,"
though not ranking with the great masters of fiction
that have been referred to, appears to have been well
informed respecting Colonial Virginia, and may be accepted as having given what is probably a fair picture
of a night in the Williamsburg theater during the Colonial period.*

One of the principal characters in the novel is a
young Virginian, Mr. Effingham, who, after a visit and
some stay at Oxford and in London, has returned to
the paternal home, Effingham Hall, in Virginia, and
whilst riding on horseback to visit a manorial estate on

* Dunlap, p. 16.

a plantation known as Riverhead, of a gentleman called
Lee, the father of two very attractive daughters, draws
up suddenly in the road, seeing a young lady on horseback in the center of it apparently awaiting his approach, who is thus described:

The lady was mounted on a tall white horse, which
stood perfectly quiet in the middle of the road, and
seemed to be docility itself, though the fiery eyes con-
tradicted the first impression. Rather would one acquainted with the singular character of horses have said
that this animal was subdued by the gentle hand of the
rider, and so laid aside, from pure affection, all his
waywardness.

The rider was a young girl about eighteen, and of
rare and extraordinary beauty. Her hair — so much
of it as was visible beneath her hood — seemed to be
dark chestnut, and her complexion was dazzling. The
eyes were large, full, and dark — instinct with fire and
softness, feminine modesty and collected firmness, the
firmness, however, predominating. But the lips were
different. They were the lips of a child — soft, guile-
less, tender, and confiding; they were purity and innocence itself, and seemed to say that however much the
brain might become hard and worldly, the heart of this
young woman never could be other than the tender
and delicately sensitive heart of a child.

She was clad in a riding-dress of pearl color, and
from the uniformity of this tint, it seemed to be a favorite with her. The hood was of silk, and the delicately gloved hand held a little ivory-handled riding-

whip, which now dangled at her side. The other
gloved hand supported her cheek; and in this position
the unknown lady calmly awaited Mr. Effingham's approach still nearer, though he was already near touch-
ing her.

Mr. Effingham took off his hat and bowed with elegant courtesy. The lady returned the inclination by
a graceful movement of the head.

"Would you be kind enough to point out the road
to the town of Williamsburg, sir?" she said, in a calm
and clear voice.

"With great pleasure, madam," replied Mr. Effingham. "You have lost your way?"

"Yes, sir, and very strangely; and as evening drew
on I was afraid of being benighted."

"You have but to follow the road until you reach
Effingham Hall, madam," he said,— "the house in the
distance yonder; then turn to the left, and you are in
the highway to town."

"Thanks, sir," the young girl said, with another calm
inclination of her head, and she touched her horse
with the whip.

"But cannot I accompany you?" asked Mr. Effingham, whose curiosity was greatly aroused, and found
his eyes, he knew not why, riveted to the rare beauty
of his companion's face; "do you not need me as a
guide?"

"Indeed, I think not, sir," she said, with the same
calmness. "Your direction is very plain, and I am
accustomed to ride by myself."

"But, really," began Mr. Effingham, somewhat

piqued, " I know it is intrusive — I know I have not the honor — "

She interrupted him with her immovable calmness.

" You would say you do not know me, and that your offer is intrusive. I believe, sir, I do not consider it so — it is very kind; but I am not a fearful girl, and need not trouble you at all."

And so bowed.

"One moment, madam," said Mr. Effingham; " I am really dying with curiosity to know you. 'T is very rude to say so, of course — but I am acquainted with every lady in the neighborhood, and I do not recall any former occasion upon which I had the pleasure — "

" It is very easily explained, sir," the young girl said.

" Madam ! "

" I do not live in the neighborhood."

" Ah ! no ? "

" And I am not a lady, sir. Does not that explain it ? "

Mr. Effingham scarcely believed his ears. These astounding words were uttered with such perfect calmness that there was no possible room to suppose that they were meant for a jest.

" You are surprised, sir," the young girl said quite simply and gravely.

" Upon my word, madam, — never have I, — really — "

" Your surprise will not last long, sir."

" How, madam ? "

" Do you ever visit the town of Williamsburg ? "

" Frequently."

"Well, sir, I think you will see me again. Now I must continue my way, having returned my sincere thanks for your kindness."

With which words, uttered in that wondrous voice of immovable calmness, the young girl again inclined her head, touched her white horse with the whip, and slowly rode out of sight.

The young man continued his journey to Riverhead; arrived there, and after an animated conversation with the two attractive young ladies, he encountered the father, a fine, portly old gentleman, who met him.

"Good morning, glad to see you."

Effingham bowed and said:

"The morning was so fine that I thought I could not spend it more agreeably than in a ride to Riverhead, sir."

"Delightful! These August days are excellent for the corn; what news?"

"Nothing, sir. I have not seen the 'Gazette.'"

"Oh, the 'Gazette' never contains any intelligence; sometimes, it is true, we hear what is going on in Parliament, but it never condescends to afford us any news from Virginia. The tobacco on the south side may be all gone to the devil for anything you read in the 'Gazette.' Here it is — an abominable sheet! Ah, I see we are to have a theatrical performance in Williamsburg next week," added the old gentleman, on glancing over the paper. "Mr. Hallam and his Virginia company of comedians — very politic that addition of Virginia — are to perform 'The Merchant of Venice,' by permission of his worship, the Mayor, at the *old* theater near the capital, he announces. Truly we are improving, really becoming civilized, in this barbarous *terra incognita*."

Mr. Effingham winced; he had more than once expressed a similar opinion of Virginia in good faith, not ironically, and the good old gentleman's words seemed directed to himself. A moment's reflection, however, persuaded him that this could not be the case; He had not visited Riverhead a dozen times since his arrival from Oxford and London, and on these occasions he never touched upon the subject of Virginia and its dreadful deficiencies.

"A play," he said; "that is really good news; but the 'Merchant of Venice,' that is not one of my acquaintances."

"Ah! you young men are wrong in giving up Will. Shakespeare for the Steeles, Addisons, and Vanbrughs. Mr. Addison's essays are very pleasant and entertaining reading, and surely there never was a finer gentleman than Sir Roger; but in the drama Will. Shakespeare distances him all to nothing."

"Let us go to the play," said Henrietta.

"Oh, yes," said Clara.

The old gentleman tenderly smoothed the bright golden hair.

"Certainly, if you wish it," he said.

"And may I request permission to accompany the party, ladies," said Mr. Effingham, languidly.

"How modest," said Henrietta, laughing; "certainly you may go, sir. You will tell us when to hiss or applaud, you know, as you are just from London."

"What a quick tongue she has," said Mr. Lee, fondly; well, we will all go, and see what the Virginia company of comedians is like; not much I fear."

At the appointed day the young man appears at Mr. Lee's mansion and the young ladies come down to meet him, the elder, Henrietta, being described as "radiant in a dress of surpassing elegance — flowered satin, yellow lace, jewels, powdered hair, with pendants and rich furbelows,— the bright beauty of her laughing face assorting well with her flashing and glittering costume," while the costume of the younger sister was more subdued, as her manner was more quiet.

A lively conversation follows, the subject of which ends with an inquiry on the part of the young man to the elder sister.

"Do you anticipate much pleasure?" referring to the play, to which the other replies:

"Oh, it will be delightful." Then to the younger, "And you, Cousin Clara, do you think that these Virginia Comedians, as they call themselves, will afford you a very pleasant entertainment?"

"Oh, yes — I am sure I shall be pleased — you know I have never seen a play."

"But read a plenty?"

"Oh, yes; and I like the 'Merchant of Venice.' The character of Portia is so delicate and noble."

"Quite true; an excellent criticism; better than anything in Congreve I think, though I should hesitate to advance such an opinion in London."

"Who will act Portia?"

" I don't know, but can tell you without much difficulty. Here is a play-bill that I sent to town for yesterday."

And Mr. Effingham drew daintily from his coat pocket a small, roughly printed hand-bill, which he spread out before the eyes of Clara.

"'Virginia Company of Comedians,'" he read, "'by permission of his worship the Mayor—in the old theatre near the capitol, on Thursday evening—a tragedy called 'The Merchant of Venice,' by Mr. William Shakespeare, boxes seven shillings sixpence'—'Vivat Rex et Regina'—here it is, 'Shylock, Mr. Rigby; Portia, Miss Beatrice Hallam.' The part of Portia is to be performed by Miss Beatrice Hallam—I have never seen or heard of her."

"Which means," said Henrietta, laughing, "that Miss Beatrice cannot be very well worth seeing, as Mr. Champ Effingham, just from London, and conversant with all the celebrities there, has never heard of her existence."

" My dear Cousin Henrietta," said Mr. Effingham, languidly, "you really seem to sit in judgment on my wearisome conversation. I do not profess to know anything about celebrities. True, I very frequently lounged into the theater in London, but I assure you took very little interest in the plays or performers. Life itself is enough of a comedy for me, and I want nothing more. I know nothing of Miss Hallam. She may be a witch of Endor, or as beautiful as Cleopatra, Queen of Egypt, for all that I know. That I have not heard her proves nothing. The best actors and actresses are often treated with neglect and indifference."

" Well," said Clara, smiling, " we soon shall see for
ourselves, for there is papa coming, all ready dressed
to go, and I hear the wheels of the chariot."

Upon which they go to the play-house, which the
novelist thus describes :

The " old theatre near the capitol," discoursed of in
the manifesto issued by Mr. Manager Hallam, was so
far old that the walls were well browned by time, and
the shutters to the windows of a pleasant neutral tint
between rust and dust color. The building had, no
doubt, been used for the present purpose in bygone
times, before the days of the " Virginia Gazette," which
is our authority for many of the facts here stated, and
in relation to the " Virginia Company of Comedians "—
but of the former companies of " players," as my Lord
Hamlet calls them, and their successes and misfortunes,
printed words tell us nothing, as far as the researches
of the present " Chronicle " extend. That there had
been such companies before, however, we repeat, there
is some reason to believe ; else why that addition " old"
applied to the " theatre near the capitol."

Within, the play-house presented a somewhat more
attractive appearance. There was " box," " pit," and
" gallery," as in our own day ; and the relative prices
were arranged in much the same manner. The common
mortals — gentlemen and ladies — were forced to oc-
cupy the boxes raised slightly above the level of the
stage and hemmed in by velvet-cushioned railings —
in front a flower-decorated panel extending all around

the house — and for this position they were moreover compelled to pay an admission fee of seven shillings and sixpence. The demigods — so to speak — occupied a more eligible portion in the "pit," from which they could procure a highly excellent view of the actors' feet and ankles, just on a level with their noses; to conciliate the demigods this superior advantage had been offered, and the price for them was further still reduced to five shillings. But "the gods," in truth, were the real favorites of the manager. To attract them he arranged the high upper "gallery" and left it untouched, unencumbered by railing, velvet cushions, or any other device; all was free space and liberal as the air; there were no troublesome seats for "the gods," and three shillings and ninepence all that the manager would demand. The honor of their presence was enough.

From the boxes a stairway led down to the stage, and some rude scenes, visible at the edges of the curtain, completed the outfit.

When Mr. Lee and his daughters entered the box, which had been reserved for them next to the stage, the house was nearly full, and the neatness of the edifice was lost sight of in the sea of brilliant ladies' faces and showy forms of cavaliers which extended, like a sea of glittering foam, around the semicircle of the boxes. The pit was occupied by well-dressed men of the lower class, as the times had it, and from the gallery proceeded hoarse murmurs and the unforgotten slang of London.

Many smiles and bows were interchanged between the parties in the different boxes and the young gallants, following the fashion of the day, gathered at each end of the stage, and often walked across, to exchange some polite speech with the smiling dames in the boxes nearest.

Mr. Champ Effingham was, upon the whole, much the most notable fop present, and his elegant *petit maître* air as he strutted across the stage attracted many remarks, not invariably favorable. It was observed, however, that when the Virginia-bred youths, with honest plainness, called him " ridiculous," the young ladies, their companions, took Mr. Effingham's part, and defended him with great enthusiasm ; but when they returned home he was more unmercifully criticized than he would otherwise have been.

A little bell rang, and the orchestra, represented by three or four foreign-looking gentlemen, bearded and moustached, entered with trumpet and violins. The trumpet made the roof shake indifferently in honor of the *Prince of Morocco*, or *King Richard*, or any other worthy whose entrance was marked in the play-book " with a flourish." But before the orchestra ravished the ears of every one, the manager came forward in the costume of *Bassanio*, and made a low bow. Mr. Hallam was a fat little man, of fifty or fifty-five, with a rubicund and somewhat sensual face, and he expressed extraordinary delight at meeting so many of the " noble aristocracy of the great and noble colony of Virginia " assembled to witness his very humble representation. " It would be the chief and sole ambition of his life," he said, " to please the gentry who so kindly patronized their servants — himself and his

associates " — and then the smiling worthy concluded
by bowing lower than before. Much applause from
the pit and gallery and murmurs of approbation from
the well-bred boxes greeted the address, and the orchestra having struck up, the curtain slowly rolled
aloft, the young gallants scattered to the corner of the
stage, seating themselves on stools or chairs or standing, and the " Merchant of Venice" commenced.
Bassanio, having assumed a dignified and lofty part,
embraced *Gratiano* with courteous and lordly art, his
friend *Antonio* offered him his fortune with grand mag-
nanimity in a loud, singing voice, worthy the utmost
commendation, and the first act proceeded on its way
in triumph.

The first act ends, the scene between *Portia* and
Nerissa being omitted, the audience being highly
pleased, and the actors receiving a " grateful guerdon
of applause." What transpires between the inmates
of the box occupied by Effingham's father and the
Squire, as he is called, is manifest, consisting mainly
of the conversation between the Squire and the local
parson that the Squire had invited to witness the play,
who sits on the front seat beside the Squire with solemn
gravity and rubicund nose, surveying from his respectable position the agitated pit.

" Not so bad as you predicted, eh, parson ? " says
the Squire. "I don't think that fellow *Antonio* acts
so badly."

" Very well — very well," is the latter's response.

" The audience seems delighted. Look at the scamp
of a son of mine, strutting up to friend Lee's box

and smoothing those enormous ruffles like a turkey cock."

Effingham leaves the companions with whom he had been seated on the stage, interchanging remarks during the performance to the great disgust of the pit, and approaching Miss Clara, who sits nearest the stage, looking very beautiful and radiant with pleasure, asks:

"And how does my fair cousin relish the performance?"

"Oh, I was never more pleased with anything. And how do you like it?"

"Tolerably. But I never had a great relish for these things."

"Because, to wit, life itself is a comedy," said Henrietta, laughing.

"Yes," replied Effingham, "and a very brilliant one it would be if all the world were Miss Henriettas. I hope, my dear cousin, the compliment is sufficiently broad."

"Thank you, sir. I know how to take your fine speeches. Don't think they deceive me."

"I'm rather a poor hand at compliments," replied Effingham; "but, really, it is hard to do you the injustice, my fair cousin, of withholding them. Come, no reply, for I see my Cousin Clara is going to say something more flattering than what you are about to utter."

"Oh, no," says Clara, slightly blushing; "I was only going to say that *Shylock* really frightened me."

"It was very well done; much like Shuter at Castle

Garden. How did you like it, Cousin Henrietta? Come, your criticism."

"Oh, what could you expect from a country girl like me?" and broke off the conversation by announcing the approach of a fox-hunter, who was an admirer.

"How I envy them," he says to Clara, applying to his nostrils, with a listless air, a delicate kind of snuff, "they are so gay."

Then after some conversation with Clara preparatory to making her the proffer of his hand, he describes his condition as "out of sorts," as "rusting."

"Yes, more than rusting — I take interest in scarcely anything; I am wearied to death — with everything. What is life worth? Here are some hundreds of persons and they all seem delighted with the play, which tires me to death. I take no interest in it. *Shylock* and *Antonio* strut and spout without amusing me. I am already weary and everybody else seems to be impatient for the reappearance of the wonders. Why are they so much amused? For my part I am sick of all this and only stay because you stay. The nearest approach to happiness I make is in your presence," at which, of course, the young lady blushes, and after this near approach he follows it up by declaring "how beautiful she is," that he really thinks that she could charm away his melancholy if she desired, upon which she asks:

"How, pray?"

"By smiling at me."

Clara smiled and said:

"Be merry then; indeed, Cousin, you could become
so again if you chose.   Do not determine to find fault
with everything and think everything means you.   Seek
novelty ; you say that all here seem to take pleasure in
the play while you do not.   They are pleased because
it is new to them.   I have never seen a play, and I am
highly pleased.   If you have been often to the theater
there is nothing strange in your thinking this poor one
excellent, though it seems beautiful to me.   But you
will find usually an interest in other things.   Try it, and
see if my philosophy is not true."

His response is that he knew but one means.

"What is that ? "

"To have a companion."

The meaning suddenly flashed upon her, and she
turned away.

"Clara, dearest Clara, if you take such an interest
in my welfare why— "

Sh-h-h-h came in a loud murmur from the audience,
the curtain having risen, which Effingham recognizes,
and ejaculates:

"How ridiculous, here in the theater."   Upon which
his eye suddenly fell upon one of the actresses, and he
almost uttered an exclamation.   It was the unknown
lady of the wood.

The novelist continues :

The unknown lady was no gentle Virginia maiden,
no "lady," as she had said with perfect calmness at their
meeting — only one of the company of comedians.
Her singular expression when she uttered the words,

" I think you will see me again," occurred to the young man, and he wondered that this easy solution of the riddle had not occurred to him at once.

" What was her name ? " Mr. Effingham drew forth his bill and saw opposite the name of *Portia*, Miss Beatrice Hallam.

" Ah, yes," he said, carelessly, " the same we were speculating upon this morning. Let us see how *Portia* looks, and what change the footlights work in her face."

He sat down in the corner of the stage upon a wicker chair and scanned *Portia* critically. Her costume was faultless. It consisted of a gown and underskirt of fawn-colored silk trimmed with silver, and a single band of gold encircled each wrist, clearly relieved against the white, finely-rounded arm. Her hair, which was a beautiful chestnut, had been carried back from the temples and powdered after the fashion of the time, and around her beautiful, swan-like neck the young woman wore a necklace of pearls of rare brilliancy. Thus the costume of the character defied criticism, and Mr. Effingham passed on to the face and figure. These we have already described. The countenance of Beatrice Hallam wore the same simple, yet firm and collected expression, which Mr. Effingham had observed in their first interview, and her figure had the same indefinable grace and beauty. Every movement which she made might have suited a royal palace, and in her large, brilliant eyes Mr. Effingham sought the least trace of confusion. She surveyed the audience, whilst the *Prince of Morocco* was uttering his speech, with perfect simplicity, but her eyes not for a single moment rested on the young men collected at the corner of the stage. For her they seemed to have no existence, and she turned to the *Prince* again. That gentleman having uttered his prescribed number of lines, *Portia* advanced graciously towards him and addressed him. Her carelessness was gone. She no longer betrayed either indifference or coldness; she was the actress, with her rôle to sustain. She commenced in a voice of noble and queen-like courtesy, a voice of pure music and clear utterance, so to speak, such as few lips possess the power of giving forth. Every word rang and told; there was no hurry, no slurring, no hesitation. It was not an actress delivering a set speech, but the noble *Portia*, doing the honors of her beautiful palace at Belmont. The scene ended with great applause — the young woman had evidently produced a most favorable impression on the audience. But she seemed wholly unconscious of this compliment, and made her exit quite calmly.

A buzz ran through the theater; the audience were discussing the merits of *Portia*. On the stage, too, she was the subject of many comments, and this continued until *Lancelot* made his appearance and went through his speech; then *Portia* reappeared with the *Prince*, and was greeted with great applause.

Mr. Effingham leaned forward and touched the young woman's sleeve.

" Come," he said with easy carelessness, and scarcely moderating his voice; " come, fair *Portia*, while that tiresome fellow is making his speech, and talk to me a little. We are old acquaintances, and you are indebted to me for directing you home."

"Yes, sir," said Beatrice, turning her head slightly; "but pardon me — I have my part to attend to."

"I don't care."

"Excuse me, sir; but I do."

"Really, madame, you are very stiff for an actress. Is it so very unusual a thing to ask a moment's conversation?"

"I know that it is the fashion in London and elsewhere, sir, but I dislike it. It destroys my conception of the character," she said, calmly.

Mr. Effingham laughed. "Come here again, and talk to me," he said. "Did you not say we should meet again?"

"Yes, sir; and I also said I was not a lady."

"Well, what is the meaning of that addition?"

"It means, sir, that being an actress I am not at liberty to amuse myself here as I might were I a lady in a drawing room. Pardon me, sir," she added, calmly, "I am neglecting what I have engaged to do — play *Portia*."

And the young woman, quietly disengaging her sleeve from Mr. Effingham's fingers, moved away to another part of the stage.

"Here is a pretty affair," said Mr. Effingham to himself, as he fell back languidly into the chair from which, however, he had not deigned to rise wholly when addressing the young actress. "What are things coming to when an actress treats a gentleman in this manner. I really believe the girl thinks I am not good enough for her. 'Pardon me, sir,' was there ever such insufferable prudery and affectation. No doubt she wishes to catch me, and commences with this piquant piece of acting, or, perhaps," added the elegant young gentleman, smoothing his frill, "she fell in love with me the other day when we met and is afraid she will betray herself. Not talk when I desire to talk with her, indeed, and yonder all of these people have seen her careless treatment of me and are laughing at me. Fortunately I am proof against these jeers. Come, come, let us see if Miss Portia will treat me as badly next time."

Portia entered next with the *Prince of Arragon,* and while that gentleman was addressing the caskets, Mr. Effingham again applied himself to the task of forcing the young woman to converse with him.

"Why did you treat me so just now?" he said, with abrupt carelessness.

"How, sir."

"You refused to talk to me."

"I had my part to perform."

"That is no excuse."

"Besides, sir," added the young woman, surveying Mr. Effingham with an indifferent glance, "I know you only very slightly."

"Know me only slightly!" said Mr. Effingham affecting surprise.

"A chance meeting is very slight acquaintance, sir; but I offer this as no apology for refusing to do what I am now doing, converse with you on the stage."

"Really, one would say you were a queen speaking to a subject instead of an actress —"

"Honored with the attentions of a gentleman, you would add, sir," she interrupted, quite calmly."

" As you please."

" Pray speak to me no more, sir. I forget my part, and the audience are looking at you."

" Let them."

" I see some angry faces," said the young woman; " they do not understand the fashions of London, sir."

" What care I."

" Please release my sleeve, sir — that is my line."

The gallery uttered a prolonged hiss as *Portia* disengaged her arm. Mr. Effingham turned around and looked up to the gallery from which the hiss came; this glance of haughty defiance might have provoked another exhibition of the same sort, but *Portia* at that moment commenced her speech.

Thereafter the young woman came no more near Mr. Effingham, and treated that gentleman's moody glances with supreme disregard. What was going on in Mr. Effingham's mind, and why did he lose some of his careless listlessness, when, clasping her beautiful hands, the lovely girl, raising her eyes to heaven like one of the old Italian pictures, uttered that sublime discourse on the " quality of mercy "; and how did it happen that she sobbed, almost, in that tender, magical voice:

> But mercy is above this sceptered sway;
> It is enthroned in the hearts of kings;
> It is an attribute of God himself.

How did it chance that Mr. Effingham led the enthusiastic applause and absolutely arose erect in the excess of his enthusiasm ?

As she passed him in going out he made her a

low bow and said, "Pardon me! You are a great actress."

The play proceeded and ended amid universal applause. Mr. Hallam led out *Portia* in response to uproarious calls, and thanked the audience for their kindness to his daughter. Beatrice received the applause with her habitual calmness, inclining her head slightly as she disappeared, and the audience separated, rolling well pleased to their homes.*

In 1886 a large quarto volume was published entitled " A History of the American Theatre before the Revolution," by George O. Seilhamer. There appeared to be no occasion for a special history of this particular period of twenty-nine years, that is from 1749 to the Revolution, as Dunlap's history extended from 1752 to about 1817, and what was known at the time of Mr. Seilhamer's publication respecting the theater in North America before 1752 had already been published in Ireland's " History of the New York Stage," and in the paper here reprinted, except one item to be referred to hereafter.

* Dunlap gives the full cast of the " Merchant of Venice," the first play enacted by the Hallam Company in America, at Williamsburg, September 5, 1752, as he received it from Lewis Hallam, Jr., by which it appears that Mrs. Hallam, the manager's wife, was the *Portia*, that Miss Hallam represented *Jessica*, "her first appearance on any stage," and an actor named Malone played *Shylock*. The author of the novel states that his wish was simply to depict some Virginia scenes and personages ten years before the Revolution, or the Virginia of 1765, and trusts that his picture is at least truthful as far as it goes, which it probably is, with the anachronism of the appearance, in the year 1765,

There were some further corrections to be made to Dunlap's history, but they were not very important or numerous, and some additional information to be added respecting theatrical performances in Maryland and Pennsylvania that was new and interesting. This was included in this special history, which, in addition to what had been previously published, was largely made up of the full casts, as they are called in theatrical parlance, of plays given at particular dates during the Colonial period; that is, the name of the performer of each part, taken from the small play-bills that are printed for the use of the audience. As it is the custom in theaters for the prompter to keep a file of these bills each season, and the habit of some persons to keep the play-bill of any performance they have seen, considerable collections of these small play-bills have been preserved, and exist in private collections or in institutions or clubs, of which Mr. Seilhamer has made copious use, and has also inserted in this volume long lists of the performances given at particular dates and tabulated statements of the leading parts of actors and

---

of Miss Hallam, a young girl of about eighteen, as *Portia*, thirteen years after she had made her first appearance on the stage in the same play as *Jessica*. But liberties of this kind are pardonable in a novelist. They are taken by great authors. Scott, in his novel of Kenilworth, the scene of which romance is laid in the year 1575, represents Lord Leicester, in passing through the court-rooms, stopping to compliment Shakespeare on the success of his recent poem of Venus and Adonis, Shakespeare being then eleven years of age. The poem was printed in 1593, eighteen years after the event described by the novelist, or when Shakespeare was twenty-nine years of age.

actresses, and the statements of performances, culled from the Colonial newspapers, by all of which insertions the volume is augmented to the magnitude of a large quarto.

Dunlap, while stating that play-bills and theatrical advertisements are of assistance, or, as he expressed it, "throw light" (that is, they may assist the historian in the construction of his narrative), evidently thought that this minute information, or detail, of this kind was not, save in exceptional instances, to be inserted bodily in a history, for he apologizes to his readers for inserting three full casts of plays that were performed in the years 1752, 53, and 54, in these words: "Particularity of this kind would be unnecessary in regard to events of more recent date and *out of place in a history of a theatre*, but in this early stage of the work before us, we think a play-bill a valuable source of information and gladly insert it," * and in this respect we incline to the opinion of Dunlap.

But Seilhamer does not. In this age of many books, the aim of able historical writers is condensation with clearness, but with him it appears to have been expansion with pledty of material; for while Dunlap, in a history extending over sixty-five years, inserts but three full casts of plays, Seilhamer, in one extending over only twenty-nine, years, inserts 253, and adds also one-fifth of that number of theatrical advertisements and numerous lists of performances at different dates, and tables of prominent performers' leading parts, which are all in-

---

* 2 Dunlap, 24, 48 : London ed.

corporated with the text, and form a part of the narrative. I apprehend that it was the chief material that he had; that he meant to supplant Dunlap as the future historian of the American Theater, and that the amount of other information that was new, that is, that had not previously been published, would have been for such a purpose so insufficient that it was necessary to swell the book out to the dimension of a large quarto with material of this kind, connected together by a slight thread of narrative; material of which there was an abundant supply, for he followed up this publication by two more of the same kind in the years 1889 and 1891, each, however, distinguished from the other by a different title, the whole ending in 1797.

To his manifest desire to supplant Dunlap there could be no objection, if he had the ability to produce a better and more interesting book. On the contrary, a history of the American Stage from the earliest knowledge we have of it to the time of publication, by a writer who had the leisure to make the necessary research, and the art so to arrange his material as to make the work reliable and readable, would be a contribution to literature. Seilhamer's opinion of what he could do, and had done, is subsequently shown by his constant abuse of Dunlap throughout these three volumes, for Dunlap's name rarely, if ever, occurs without his applying to it some derogatory, contemptuous, or other abusive epithet. Such as the "marvelous chronicler," "the quality of blundering for which he was remarkable," or some like term or phrase to belittle him. He says in respect to his history, that "never

was a book written to throw light upon a subject that
so completely confused it." "His dates are always
wrong." "He presents to the world the remarkable
example of a man who wrote the annals of the American Stage from some scattered memoranda, and out
of his own head," and refers to the "readiness of
assumption he was apt to resort to in the absence of
facts," "the consequences of which are" he says,
"that the stream of American theatrical history was
poisoned at its source"; that "his inaccuracies are so
many and so unreasonable that it is impossible not to
wonder at the mental equipment of a man that could
be guilty of them." "His statements of facts are"
declared to be "always misstatements in whole or
in part." He finds him "inexcusable for not knowing the date of the first appearance of a certain
actress and for his want of knowledge of an early
American play." He is declared to have been a failure in everything; as an historian, a novelist, an artist, a theatrical manager, and as a dramatist. A drama
of his is a failure for the want of skill in the management of the plot, and the insufficiency of the characters
and the incidents; another is disposed of as a " turgid
melodrama without action"; all his plays and adapta-
tions of plays are condemned as having passed into de-
served oblivion; but as regards the history something
had to be conceded, and it is therefore said that, "full of
mistakes as it is — mistakes for which it is impossible to
forgive him," it has some features that commend it;
such as the account he was able to give from personal
knowledge of the players that were on the American

stage in the first quarter of the century after the Revolution, which it is conceded "the world could ill afford to
lose," and might well be conceded, as it is more interesting than anything in Seilhamer's three volumes. But
even this is qualified by his saying, in respect to the Dunlap Society being named after him, that "there probably never was a writer less deserving of such an honor
than Dunlap," that his plays were "without merit,
either for stage represention or as literary productions,
and that his history was "at once dull and inaccurate,"
with the further observation that he "might have been
looked upon as an interesting character, had he not
been at once jealous and abusive of every one outside
of his circle of friends, ignoring the efforts of others
not inferior to his own."

It may be said of this array of accusations against
Dunlap that, except in some matters of little importance,
they are merely Seilhamer's own conclusions or assumptions, and derive no additional weight from any facts
stated in his volumes. It is a literary mistake for an
historical writer to indulge in such continued abuse as
this of a previous writer on the same subject. If the first
historian has made errors or mistakes, it is sufficient
quietly to correct them; but to constantly abuse and
belittle him is objectionable and offensive on the part
of the second, for it is continually reiterating his own
superiority and importance as an historian.

It is especially so in this writer, for he is as prone to
indulge in conjectures or assumptions that afterward
prove to be unfounded, as he asserts Dunlap is, and in
matters quite as important; with this difference, that,

when he refers to anything of this kind on the part of
Dunlap, it is stigmatized as "the blunder of an ignorant
historian," one example of which will suffice. When
Dunlap stated that it was the Hallam Company that first
introduced the drama in America, he also stated that
this was communicated to him by one of that company,
Lewis Hallam, Jr., and which he might reasonably suppose to be true, coming, as it did, from one of that company; but when Seilhamer states that "the history of the
drama in this country may be said to begin with the
production of Addison's 'Cato' in Philadelphia in
August, 1749," he does so upon the authority only of the
item before referred to, which is an entry in a manuscript
journal kept by one John Smith of Philadelphia, of the
date of August 12, 1749, recording that Smith had been
at a friend's house whose daughter was going, as one
of a company, to hear the tragedy of "Cato," which
at that time was the earliest reference known to the
performance of a play in the American Colonies, and
which Seilhamer assumed to have been the commencement of the drama in this country. Now it had been
previously shown in the paper here reprinted, that there
was a play-house in New York in 1733, sixteen years
before. This interfered with such a conclusion, and as
he could not avoid referring to this fact, he did so very
boldly, declaring that "as an attempt to transplant the
drama to the Colonies, it had no effect upon the development of the American stage," giving this opinion
respecting a period. of which he knew nothing, for we
now know that many years before this performance
of "Cato" in Philadelphia, there were play-houses in

had not been for exertions of this nature on his part, a large portion of the early history of the American theater which is interesting would have been lost. He was also the historian of the arts of design in this country, which embraced an account of our painters, from William Watson in 1715 to William Page in 1832, which is full of material not elsewhere found, and which no one was so competent to gather as himself. He wrote a history of the State of New York, which, in the continuation of the narrative to the time of publication, supplied a want that it still continues to supply; and while, as a portrait painter, he was neither a Stuart nor a Jarvis, he was at least a respectable limner, and the statement of Seilhamer that " he painted numerous portraits with sketches of his theatrical contemporaries, most of them wretched caricatures," is but an exhibition of the writer's ignorance or of his malevolence.

The Dunlap Society was formed for the printing of papers connected with the history of the American theater, or reprinting what had become scarce upon that subject and was worth preserving. Societies of a like general nature have been formed in England and in this country, which have usually been named after some individual who at an early period was prominently identified with the subject matter in which the society is interested; and when what has been here stated respecting Dunlap is considered, with the fact that he was the first historian of the American theater, and the purpose for which the Dunlap Society was formed, it appears to me that the choice of his name for it was as appropriate, if not more so, than that of any other American of that period.

The concluding illustration is a facsimile of the oldest American play-bill as far as known, the original of which is in the possession of Mr. Thomas J. McKee of New York.   It is thought worthy of insertion as a curiosity, and not as approving Mr. Seilhamer's extensive use of such material, which, he says, is "introduced as a part of the record which it is the aim of this work to preserve with as much completeness as possible," and again, that "the monument of the actors is the record of their work in the newspapers," and it is due in justice to him to state that in the two later volumes, and especially in the third, there is much information that is new and interesting, the result, evidently, of a very thorough examination of the Colonial and other newspapers until within a few years of the commencement of the present century.

By a Company of COMEDIANS,

At the New-Theatre, in *Naſſau-Street*,

This Evening, being the 12th of *November*, will be preſented,

(By particular Deſire)

An *Hiſtorical Play*, call'd,

King RICHARD III.

CONTAINING

The Diſtreſſes and Death of King *Henry* the VIth ; the artful
Acquiſition of the Crown by *Crook-back'd Richard* ; the Murder
of the two young Princes in the Tower ; and the memorable
Battle of *Boſworth-Field*, being the laſt that was fought between
the Houſes of *York* and *Lancaſter*.

Richard,	by	Mr. *Rigby.*
King *Henry*,	by	Mr. *Hallam.*
Prince *Edward*,	by	Maſter *L. Hallam.*
Duke of *York*,	by	Maſter *A. Hallam.*
Earl of *Richmond*,	by	Mr. *Clarkſon.*
Duke of *Buckingham*,	by	Mr. *Malone.*
Duke of *Norfolk*,	by	Mr. *Miller.*
Lord *Stanley*,	by	Mr. *Singleton.*
Lieutenant,	by	Mr. *Bell.*
Cateſby,	by	Mr. *Adcock.*
Queen *Elizabeth*,	by	Mrs. *Hallam.*
Lady *Anne*,	by	Mrs. *Adcock.*
Ducheſs of *York*,	by	Mrs. *Rigby.*

To which will be added,

A Ballad F A R C E call'd,

The *DEVIL TO PAY.*

Sir *John Loverule*,	by	Mr. *Adcock.*
Jobſon,	by	Mr. *Malone.*
Butler,	by	Mr. *Miller.*
Footman,	by	Mr. *Singleton.*
Cook,	by	Mr. *Bell.*
Coachman,	by	Mr. *Rigby.*
Conjurer,	by	Mr. *Clarkſon.*
Lady *Loverule*,	by	Mrs. *Adcock.*
Nell,	by	Mrs. *Becceley.*
Lettice,	by	Mrs. *Clarkſon.*
Lucy,	by	Miſs *Love.*

PRICES : BOX, 6ſ. PIT, 4ſ. GALLERY, 2ſ.

No Perſons whatever to be admitted behind the Scenes.

N. B. *Gentlemen and Ladies that chuſe Tickets, may have them
at Mr.* Parker's *and Mr.* Gaine's *Printing-Offices.*

Money will be taken at the DOOR.

To begin at 6 o'Clock.

A CONSIDERATION OF THE OBJECTIONS
MADE TO THE STAGE.

THIS supplement began with the statement that among the earliest information that we possess respecting the drama in America, is a passage in a letter objecting to the performance of a play, and it may be appropriately closed by a brief enumeration of the objections generally made to the theater, and the conclusion that seems to follow from a review of them.

It is a characteristic of those who object to the theater altogether that they rarely, if ever, give any consideration to the origin of the drama, to its long continuance, or appreciate that it will continue as long as civilization continues, and this applies as well to those who have written elaborate treatises against it, like Jeremy Collier, as to those who object to it generally. The briefest form of stating this consideration is that the theater has its origin in human nature. In the researches made as to its origin it is found that it has sprung up spontaneously among different peoples, and has not been transmitted by one people more advanced in civilization to another that was less so. Thus the rise of the drama, such as it is, in India and in China has in no way been influenced by the Greeks, who carried the cultivation of it to a higher degree than any other people of antiquity. The oldest civilization with which we are acquainted is that of Egypt. Whether it existed among the Egyptians, whether they had what we call a theater, the extensive researches that have been made within the present century so far as I have been able to ascertain do not indicate,* but that it existed at a very early period in China, in Persia, and in India we have ample evidence, and in China and India it has from its beginning been a recreation greatly enjoyed by the people; to which may be added as a general observation that certain races have more aptitude for the enjoyment of it than others, and greater natural capacity either as a gift from nature or for acquiring what is requisite in the actor or dramatist. That some men are endowed by nature in a higher degree than others with the qualities that make a man eminent as a dramatist or an actor is sufficiently indicated in the one case by Shakespeare, and in the other by Garrick, of the latter of whom it may be said, in the language of Mr. Baker, the historian of the London stage, that "without ˈany previous apprenticeship, preparation, or drudgery, at a remote end of the town that had hitherto been as unknown to fashion as the wilds of Africa, without preliminary puffing of any kind,

---

* I consulted Dr. Dickerman, the most eminent Egyptologist in this country, upon this subject, and his observation was this: The state of mind and the condition of society of the ancient Egyptians were not such as would incline them to theatrical representations. They had athletic sports, games, such as draughts or checkers, and games of chance, but not such a disposition as brought people together to witness anything. None of the buildings whose ruins have been studied indicate that any were constructed with reference to the assembling of people, except the processions, with priests, in the temples, and that the Labyrinth, moreover, in the twelfth dynasty, contemporary with Abraham, had meetings of the delegates from the different nomes, or provinces, to discuss the political affairs of the kingdom.

he took the whole play-going public by storm, made
men old in prejudice forget the idols of their youth and
like Pope confess that he never had his equal. * * *
From " Richard III." to " Abel Drugger," from " King
Lear" to " Don Felix," from " Macbeth " to "Bayes," his
tragic force, his keen sense of humor, his marvelous
genius carried everything before it;" and this combina-
tion of equal excellence, and in the highest degree, in both
tragedy and comedy is the more remarkable, for the
two great Roman actors, Roscius in comedy and
Æsopus in tragedy, never crossed the limits of their
respective branches, and both reached the preëminence
they attained by the most careful and assiduous study.
It is said of Roscius that, in the very height of his
reputation, he did not even venture upon a gesture that
he did not carefully consider and practise in private,
and yet, notwithstanding this elaborate study, there was
no mannerism or affectation in his acting, but everything he did seemed natural to the character he represented ; and having referred to these two great Roman
actors, it may be mentioned, as an example of being
endowed like Garrick with qualities that enable him
who possesses them to soar easily and at once to the
highest reach of his art, that Terence, the most elegant, subtle, and felicitous in expression of the Roman
comic dramatists, is supposed, his biography being but
imperfectly known, to have been born a slave, who at
the age of twenty-seven offered his first play, the " An-
dria," to the conductors of the theatrical exhibitions,
who referred him to an eminent playwright of Rome
for its examination, where, unknown and meanly clad,

he read, seated upon a low stool, his opening scene, afterwards declared by Cicero to be a model of narrative, and his genius was at once recognized.*

Cæsar called him a half Menander, who was the Greeks' ideal of a perfect comic dramatist, regarding him in comedy, as they did Sophocles in tragedy, as the most complete and finished; whose judgment we accept, as no play of Menander, though he is said to have written about a hundred comedies, has come down to us, but only fragments.   And Plautus, the other distinguished Roman dramatist, should also be mentioned as a further illustration, for he left the humble employment of turning a mill to become a writer of plays, and surpassed Terence in native comic force, his gift in that direction being as great as Shakespeare's or Molière's.

There is one pervading feature of the drama to which those who have written against it seldom refer, and some of the most prominent not at all, that the stage is, what the age is, or, as Shakespeare has succinctly expressed it in *Hamlet's* speech to the players, "that the purpose of playing, both at the first and now, was and is, as 't were, to hold the mirror up to nature; to show virtue her own feature, scorn her own image, and the *very age* and body of the time his form and *pressure*," and to *Polonius*, in respect to the players, that "they are the abstract and brief chronicles of the time."

If a people are alike brave and greatly cultivated, as the Athenians were when the drama reached to its high-

* Smith's Dictionary, Vol. iii, p. 997.

est attainment among them, they witness with pleasure the reproduction of noble deeds, and listen with
delight to the inculcation of noble sentiments from
such masters of the dramatic art as Euripedes and
Sophocles, and realize with great enjoyment the power
that lies in ridicule as a means of reforming public
abuses and correcting deformities in the character of
individuals when it comes from such a satirist and wit
as Aristophanes. But when a nation is sinking into decay
or deteriorating, the stage deteriorates with it; or when a
people find their highest enjoyment in amusements that
are coarse or brutal, like the Romans, who thronged the
amphitheater to witness the sanguinary combat of
gladiators, the "maddening excitement of the circus"; *
or found pleasure in such a spectacle as beholding the
arena filled with wild beasts, tearing each other to
pieces — the performances of the theater, though of a
different kind, became, in time, of the like degraded
character, and stirred up against the drama its greatest, longest, and most unrelenting enemy — the Chris-

* Gibbon says the Roman people considered the circus as
their home, their temple, and the seat of the republic. The impatient crowd rushed at the dawn of day to secure their places ;
and there were many who passed sleepless and anxious nights in the
adjacent porticos. From the morning to the evening, careless of the
sun or of the rain, the spectators, who sometimes amounted to
the number of four hundred thousand, remained in eager attention ; their eyes fixed on the horses and charioteers, their minds
agitated with hope and fear, for the success of the colors which
they espoused and the happiness of Rome appeared to hang on
the event of a race. " Gibbon's Decline and Fall," Vol. iv. pp. 87,
88. London edition of 1848.

tian Church. A warfare against it, at that time, on the part of the Church, that was necessary for the preservation of society; for in the period which Gibbon, in his great contribution to English literature, distinguishes as the Decline and Fall of the Roman Empire, the stage sank lower than it ever was before, or has ever been since.

St. Augustine, writing in the beginning of the fourth century, in an article of great severity against the theater, with whose abuses he was no doubt thoroughly familiar in his wild youth, says: " The theaters, those cages of uncleanliness and public schools of debauchery, are tumbling almost everywhere," which was the fact, as stationary places of amusement in cities or towns. And Tertullian, who wrote at the end of the second century, says even the very magistrates who abet the stage discountenance the players, stigmatize their character, and cramp their freedom. " The whole tribe of them," he says, " is thrown out of all power and privilege. They are neither suffered to be lords or gentlemen, to come within the Senate, or to harangue the people." * And yet the Church, with all its efforts and all the power the law gave it, could not suppress the players, for so deeply implanted is the love for the dramatic art, alike in those whose vocation it is to represent it and those who find enjoyment in seeing it, that it continued thereafter, in some form or other, under the names of mimes, masques, drolls, and other titles, to be exhibited throughout the

* Collier, 256, 1st. ed.

different countries of Europe by a strolling class of itinerants, under the various names of gleemen, minstrels, joculators, and other titles, on the village green, in the hall or courtyard of the castle, in the city street,— a movable stage for the players being all that was necessary,— and especially at the fairs, those gatherings of the Middle Ages for commercial purposes, when amusement was one of the attractions, whether it was a local fair in a town, or one of those gatherings of people from many countries as at Beaucaire, in France.

But while the Church did not and could not suppress the practitioner, as he was then called, of the "gay science," it made him, for more than a thousand years, a wanderer and a vagabond. The consolation which religion affords to support us in our trials, cares, and troubles in this life was denied him, except so far as he could find it solely within himself; for he could participate in none of those rites or acts of religious observance which the Church administers, and the believer relies on, for securing a happy life hereafter. Upon his death-bed no mark was made upon his forehead as the Church's signet of his repentance and hope of redemption, nor could he lie in consecrated ground. If a woman who had been baptized married a player, she was excommunicated; and so were any of the laity who went to any such performances on a Sunday or a holiday, these being the only days when the working classes, after doing their duty by attending mass, had leisure for recreation.

After several centuries the Church, with a sagacity it has frequently shown, finding that it could not suppress the players — that in all countries they had the countenance and support of the common people, who, unable to acquire knowledge by reading, except in very rare instances, quickly comprehended a dramatic representation, and that it made a great impression upon them,— determined to make use of the very thing it had continued to denounce for centuries,— a play, as an instrument in the hands of the Church for spreading and more deeply impressing religion upon the unlettered classes, who then constituted the great bulk of the community, by a representation, through its instrumentality, of the miracles that had been wrought for the faith. This afterwards was extended to the representation of the passion of Christ and religious subjects generally, not only what appertained to the history of the Church but to what was theological, under the titles of miracle plays, mysteries, and moralities, to which a recent writer has felicitously given the general name of the monastic drama.*   This resort to plays as a means of religious teaching was especially the case from the tenth to the twelfth century.   Monasteries and convents, where the name of a play had been previously an abomination, now became active centers in the production, preparation, and representation of these mysteries and moralities on the part of monks and nuns.   They were written and acted by ecclesiastics, and when they were given — as they frequently were — in churches, a bishop presided at the performance, with his miter on and pastoral staff in hand.   Even nuns wrote plays, the Benedictine

* Prof. A. W. Ward.

nun Hrotsvith, of Saxony, in the tenth century, being celebrated for her plays, which were distinguishable for their purity in respect to religion and morals, her knowledge of human nature, and the dramatic interest she could impart to a scene. As the object was to attract the common people as much as possible, and to do this it was necessary to amuse and interest as well as to instruct them, these representations were not limited to the serious or solemn, but were freely interspersed with what was comic or amusing. When the devil, and his attendant, named Vice, two characters that were frequently represented in the action of the play, were confounded by some witty retort, made ridiculous by a happy thrust of humor, or were outwitted in their design by some clever trick, it may be assumed that the sleek friar and the kindly nun laughed as heartily as any of the audience. In the tenth century a miracle play called "The Deluge" was performed, in which Noah's wife refuses to go into the ark,—being represented, as it would appear, as regarding it only as a shower,— and boxes her husband's ears when he attempts to compel her to; this display of feminine pertinacity being what in theatrical parlance is regarded as a hit. And in the twelfth century the Merchant Drapers' Company of London represented in a miracle play the Creation, and, that the representation might be exact, our first parents appeared on the stage without any covering whatever, which the Drapers' Company, I suppose, regarded as appropriately illustrating the necessity for that which the merchant draper supplies; for I remember that at the celebration in 1825 in New York of the completion of the Erie Canal the tailors marched in that great procession with a huge banner, in which Adam and Eve were represented in a like condition, with the words beneath, " Ye were naked and we clothed you."

The first theater in modern times, by which I mean a permanent structure for such a purpose, in a fixed place, was erected in Paris about the year 1400, by a body known as the Confraire de la Passion de N. S., for the representation of the Scriptural mysteries. But solemn as was the name given by the founders and their purpose in building this theater, it would appear that in the course of time it had to yield to the comic and the amusing, as much, and probably more than the miracle plays, mysteries and moralities that had been long established, for in the middle of the next century, that is in 1547, it was suppressed by the Parliament for the scandal it created by what Hallam calls " this devout buffoonery."

These religious plays, however limited, extended, or different they may have been, it appears to be conceded, gave rise to the modern drama, and I think it very possible that the existence of the comic and the tragic in the same play, which we find so marked in Shakespeare, and which is so much nearer to what takes place in life than the French classical drama of Corneille and Racine, may have been suggested to Shakespeare by these early religious plays in which both were combined, which he may frequently have witnessed, and probably did, as a boy.

But although this use of the drama was an aid to

the Church, that circumstance in no way affected or lessened the Church's attitude toward the players who acted profane plays, farces, interludes, or gave any kind of dramatic entertainment of that description. It was right to employ it on behalf of the Church, but to make any other use of it was sinful and unlawful. So the player, or common player, as he was called, to distinguish him from the histrionic assistant of the Church, remained as he was before. So late even as the thirty-ninth year of Elizabeth's reign, a statute was passed declaring that common players should be taken and adjudged to be rogues, vagabonds, and sturdy beggars, etc., etc., and be subject to the penalties therein provided, which Jeremy Collier declares were " infamous to the last degree, and capital, too, unless they give over," that is, were punishable with death. But a reservation was made in favor of players that belonged to a baron or other personage of high degree, who were authorized to play under his signature and seal, by which an opening was left for the rise and development of the great era in the dramatic history of England that followed.

Notwithstanding, however, the persecution, penalties, hardships, and sufferings to which the common players were subject, they clung to their vocation with a tenacity that showed how strong was their affection for it; that it was not only a means of livelihood, but the one of all others they preferred, for to impart pleasure is as much of an enjoyment as to receive it. But persistent as was this degradation of the players, the Church and the law had to yield at last to the in-

evitable. But how long this was in coming about, or
how long the effect of it prevented the player from
being recognized as on the same level with the rest of
his fellow-men, may be illustrated by the well-known
anecdote of Garrick, when a chimney-sweep called
out to his fellow, " There goes Garrick the player," and
his companion responded, " Hush, you don't know
what you may come to yourself."

When we examine those treatises that have been
written against the stage, the material upon which they
rely is almost invariably derived from its abuse, without considering that that abuse is not due to the theater as an institution, but to the state of society that
gives rise to it. Some writers are broad-minded
enough to make this discrimination; but the bulk of
them do not, which this contrast will sufficiently illus-
trate. Tertullian, writing about the beginning of the
third century, writes thus of the stage : " What, though
the performance may be in some measure pretty and
entertaining — what, though innocence, yes, and virtue, too, shines through some part of it! It is not the
custom to prepare poison unpalatable, nor make up
ratsbane with rhubarb and senna. No, to have the
mischief speed, they must oblige the senses and make
the dose pleasant. Thus, the devil throws in a cordial
drop to make the draught go down, and steals some
ingredients from the dispensary of heaven. In short,
look upon all the engaging sentences of the stage —
their flights of fortitude and philosophy, the loftiness of
their style, the music of the cadence, and the fineness
of the conduct! Look upon it only, I say, as honey

dropping from the bowels of a toad, or the bag of a spider."* And fourteen hundred years afterward a discrimination was made in a sermon by Archbishop Tillotson, one of the most eminent of English divines, denouncing the licentiousness of the English stage as it then existed, and the plays that were acted, as a reproach to the nation, which was true; but in which he says that to denounce the stage in general would not be just or reasonable; for, he continues, " it is very possible that they " (the plays) " might be so framed, and governed by such rules as not only to be innocently diverting, but instructing and useful; to put some vices and follies out of countenance, which cannot, perhaps, be so decently reproved nor so effectually exposed and corrected in any other way." But examples like Tillotson's, at least in England, have been rare. Even the great Bossuet, as he has been called, one of, if not the most distinguished of, French pulpit orators, and a prominent theological writer, was an example of the opposite. An actor having some scruples of conscience respecting his continuing in his profession, consulted a priest named Caffaro, who, by his reasoning, appears not only to have removed the actor's scruples, but wrote a defense of the stage, which, not being desirous of being known as the author, he published anonymously; and when it was ascertained that he was the writer of it, the Archbishop of Paris threatened to suspend him; and Bossuet wrote a pastoral letter exhorting him to repent his mistake, and rescind his

* Jeremy Collier's " View of the English Stage," 1st ed., p. 258.

mischievous opinions, which the priest accordingly did.*

While the stage may and does much to maintain a healthy moral feeling in society, in the powerful effect that is produced by the dramatic representation of virtuous deeds and of guilty actions, and the consequences that attend the latter, as an institution the theater does not retard society in its downward course, but may be said rather to accelerate it. The players depend for their support upon public patronage, and therefore court public favor, as when a nation through luxury, or those causes that bring about national decay and the consequences that follow it, or where a reaction takes place, as it did in England from the reign of puritanism to the restoration of the monarchy under Charles II., and from the example set by the restored monarch, society, or rather what is called high society, as a class, becomes corrupt and licentious, the theater caters to the taste of those who are its chief patrons, as the theaters did then by the production and representation mainly of comedies in which, as Dr. Johnson expressed it, " the plot was an intrigue, and the wit indecency," and, as respects some of these comedies, indecency might be extended to the word filth.

That great epoch that is distinguished as the Elizabethan drama, which includes some of the highest efforts of the human intellect, is embraced within the narrow limits of fifty-five years — or from Marlowe to

* Bossuet's Works, Vol. xxxii. Calcraft's " Defence of the Stage," p. 12.

Shirley — that is, from the first representation of Marlowe's "Tamerlane," in 1587, to the year 1642, when the act of Parliament was passed forbidding the acting of plays in any part of England, upon which Shirley ceased to write. It would seem to have begun to decline in Ben Jonson's life, for in the dedication to his play of "The Fox" he says at that date, 1607, respecting the theater, "that nothing but ribaldry, profanation, and blasphemy was practised," and in respect to himself, that he could with a clear conscience affirm that he "loathed the use of such foul and unwashed bawdry as is now made the food of the scene." *

However this may have been, the condition of the stage had become such as to arouse the opposition of the puritans, and in 1633 William Prynne, a puritan barrister of Lincoln's Inn, published a large volume which he called "Histrio-Mastix. The Players' Scourge, or the Actors' Tragedy, in two books, in which it is largely evidenced by divers arguments that popular stage plays are sinful, heathenish, lewd, and ungodly spectacles," a book more remarkable for the extensive erudition of the author, or rather for his industry in bringing such a mass of materials together, than for his arguments, which I shall not pause now to enumerate, as they can be considered hereafter with those of subsequent writers in the concrete, being all of the same general character, and founded almost exclusively upon the abuses of the stage.

He was persecuted by the government for the pub-

* Gifford's "Jonson," Vol. iii., pp. 162, 163.

lication of this work and heavily punished, not so much, it was said, for what he had written against the stage, as for passages in it that it was assumed were intended to reflect upon Charles I. and his queen, Henrietta Maria. The queen and her ladies had taken part in the performance of a play, and a passage in the book reflecting upon actresses in general was construed as an aspersion upon her, and a reference to Nero and other tyrants who had failed to suppress the plays was supposed to have been aimed at the king. He was tried in the Star Chamber and sentenced to be put in the pillory, to have his ears cut off and be branded on the cheek with the letters S. L. (signifying Seditious Libeller), expelled from Lincoln's Inn, deprived of his degree in the University of Oxford, and his book was ordered to be burned by the common hangman, to all of which was added a fine of £5,000, a large sum at that day, and be imprisoned for life, all of which was vigorously carried out as far as it could be. Upon the overthrow of Charles I. he was released by Parliament, the sentence against him was declared to have been illegal, a sum of money was voted to him by way of restitution, and, being a great favorite with the people, alike from his sufferings and his writings, he was elected a member of Parliament, where, strangely enough, he became a strong antagonist of Cromwell and was in turn imprisoned by his own party, became an advocate for the monarchy, was rewarded after the Restoration by the office of Keeper of the Records of the Tower, and dedicated one of his works to Charles II.

He is said to have written more than two hundred

books, a remarkable instance of fecundity, though many were, as I suppose, mere tracts or pamphlets. And this curious incident in the history of literature in respect to one of them, his work against the stage, "Histrio-Mastix," may be mentioned: that sixteen years after it was published, that is in 1649, the year in which Charles I. was executed, an unknown writer, with a view of depriving it of whatever influence it may have had, published a book entitled "William Prynne, His Defence of Stage Plays, a Retraction of a former work of his called Histrio-Mastix." It would, indeed, have been curious if a man who had written so bitterly as he had against the stage, and had accumulated and printed such a mass of learning to support the attack upon it, should have retracted all he had said and come out as the author of a work in defense of the stage. But it was a forgery; Prynne published afterwards what is called a broadside, entitled "Mr. Prynne's Vindication of himself from being the author of The Defence of Stage Plays."

It will not be necessary in a brief review like this to refer to what many eminent men have said in favor of the stage, as my purpose has been to consider the objections made against it, and it is the less necessary as it has already been admirably done by John W. Calcraft, manager of the Theater Royal of Dublin, in a volume entitled "A Defence of the Stage," published in that city in 1839. Calcraft was not only a manager of a theater, but a man with a large amount of information respecting the history of the drama, and a good classical scholar, who was able to consult the authorities when requisite in the original. He prefixes at the beginning of the book a list of those he cites or quotes in it in favor of the stage, which, independent of literary men and other writers, contains four cardinals, nine archbishops, fourteen bishops, and forty-six divines, and among them are some of the most eminent names in the church, as St. Thomas Aquinas, called the Angelic Doctor, Albertus Magnus, St. Antoninus, Archbishop of Florence, Melanchthon, and Martin Luther, the latter of whom writes: " of all amusements the theater is the most profitable"; and it further appears, on the authority of Baker's Biographia Dramatica, that more than one hundred clergymen in England have written plays. Calcraft also gives a remarkable illustration of an attempt to carry out what writers against the stage have earnestly advocated, the entire suppression of the theater, as if all mankind were made like themselves, or were capable of being made so. Charles Borromeo, Archbishop of Milan, in his zeal for the security of the public morals, " shut up the play-house and expelled the players, strollers, and minstrels as debauchers and corrupters of mankind, but soon had reason to alter his opinion, for he found that the people ran into all manner of excesses, and that, wanting something to amuse them, they committed the most horrid crimes by way of pastime. On this account he repented of his edict, recalled the banished players, and granted them a free use and liberty of the stage."

The licentiousness of the theater after the Restoration had become such as to call for some leading mind to appeal to the body of the English people, who were then, as they have always been, a strong race to bestir themselves in the cause of public morality, and such a one was found in the Rev. Jeremy Collier, a man of learning and ability, who, in 1698, published what he called "A Short View of the Immorality and Profanity of the English Stage, together with the Sense of Antiquity upon this Argument," which brought about a reformation as rapid as it was thorough. About one half the book was devoted to the English stage as it then existed, and its contrast with that of antiquity, very much to the discredit of the former, and to those who were then thought so highly of as comic dramatists. Collier was a fine classical scholar, and so familiar with the Greek dramatists and with Terence and Plautus among the Romans, as well as with all the leading comedies produced after the Restoration, that he was able to compare these comedies, passage by passage, with the Latin and Greek dramatists, and thereby furnish unanswerable proof, not only of their inferiority, but of the degraded character of the plays then produced on the English stage, when compared with the productions of the Greek and Roman dramatists. He showed in respect to the stage, in different chapters, its immodesty, its profaneness, its ridicule of the clergy, and its encouragement of immorality so completely that there was no replying to it. Dryden, who was a leading playwright at the time, yielded at once, not attempting to defend himself; on the contrary, he even thanked Collier for his treatment of him, complaining only of his roughness. Congreve undertook to reply, but it was a failure, and that he felt that

Collier was right appears in the fact that in a subsequent edition of his plays he left out many offensive
passages.

Collier's strength lay in the truth of what he said
about the condition of the English stage at that time,
and in the fact that he was a learned man, which, in
itself, inspired respect, and enabled him to cope with
any general scholar who should attempt to answer
him. The result was, that his book aroused the people, and the nation went with him in effecting a reform that has lasted ever since.

But he did not confine himself to the immorality
and profanity of the English stage, but extended his
attack to the stage in general. He devoted the latter
part of his book to copious quotations from pagan
writers, from the fathers of the church, and from the
laws that had to be passed respecting plays, to show, as
he expressed it, that they " had generally been looked
upon as the nurseries of vice, the corrupters of youth,
and the grievance of the country where they are suffered." It was my impression at first that a man so
thoroughly well informed respecting the history of the
theater in antiquity could discriminate between its use
and its abuse as its condition was then in England, and
that he made his assault upon it general that it might
have more effect than if he admitted any qualification
whatever, in the expectation that its chief patrons, who
were then what are called the higher classes, would
cease to attend the representation of these comedies
whose immorality and profaneness he had so unan-
swerably shown, and that in time by this means the

theater would gradually correct itself. But a more careful perusal of the book, and a consideration of the labor he bestowed in getting together whatever he could find from any source against it as an institution, show that his aim was the impossible — to abolish the theater altogether — that he was in full accord with the pithy St. Augustine that sinners "fancy the world goes wonderfully well when people make a figure; when a man is a prince in his fortune and a beggar in his virtue; has a great many fine things about him, but not so much as one good quality to deserve them; when the play-house goes up and religion goes down; when prodigality is admired and charity is laughed at; when the players can revel with a rich man's purse and the poor man has scarcely enough to keep soul and body together"; and with St. Hierom in his caution to ladies to have "nothing to do with the play-house, because it sets all humors at work, caresses the fancy, and makes pleasure a conveyance to destruction."

Collier divides this portion of his subject into three parts: the opinion of philosophers, orators, poets, and historians of antiquity; the opinion of the church; and that of the state as shown in the laws enacted against theaters. In making these quotations he frequently does what some advocates do, quotes so much as supports his argument and omits what qualifies or limits it. Thus, when he quotes from Plutarch that plays are dangerous to corrupt young people, and when they grow bawdy or licentious they should be checked, he omits the further observation of the great biographer, that he thought plays useful to polish the manners and instil the principles of virtue,* and, while giving what Cicero says of licentious plays as an authority against the institution of the theater, makes no mention of the fact that Roscius was an intimate friend of Cicero, and that it is to Cicero we are chiefly indebted for our knowledge of the greatness of the Roman actor and of the purity of his private life.

In considering the objections that have been made to the stage, it will not be necessary to particularize them, as they are founded almost entirely upon its abuses, in respect to which it is sufficient to say that nearly all things have their abuses; and, as Calcraft put it, to insist that the stage should be abolished and its *use* denied because of its *abuse* would be about as reasonable as to denounce the pulpit because there have been rebellious and heterodoxical preachers; to proscribe the bench because there have been corrupt and unjust judges, and periods of the venal administration of the judiciary; or dispense with the art of printing because by its means immoral books have been circulated. This will dispense with the necessity of enumerating the objections made by subsequent writers, such as the Rev. Arthur Bedford, Bossuet, Witherspoon, Law, and a few others, the first of whom, Bedford, published, in 1719, what he called "A Serious Remonstrance in behalf of the Christian Religion against the horrid blasphemies, and impurities, which are still used in the English Playhouses, being a new edition of the Evil of Stage Plays," in which he is said to have cited seven thousand lewd

* Calcraft, p. 61.

and criminal passages out of plays of the then current century, displaying, in my opinion, rather a prurient curiosity than a labor on behalf of public morality, on the part of a clergyman who might have been better employed; and as respects what has been advanced by other writers against the theater as an institution, that is concisely, energetically, and fully expressed in Collier's final conclusion, the whole of which I shall not give in detail, but sufficient to state what it was.

"My conclusion," he says, "is let nobody go to the Infamous *Play House*, A place of such staring contradiction to the Strictness and Sobriety of Religion A Place hated by God and haunted by the Devil. Let no man I say learn to relish any thing that's said there; For 'tis all but poison handsomely prepared." He objects to plays as "dilating so much on the passion of love, which is a cunning way of stealing on the blind side and practising upon the weakness of human nature," that "people love to see their passions painted no less than their persons, that recommends the business of amours and engages inclination. It forms passions where it does not find them. Love has a parley within, and when the wax is prepared the impression is easily made, and when these passions are born they thrive extremely in that nursery. They grow strong, and when the passions are up in arms there is a mighty contest between duty and inclination." He further objects to plays as encouraging the passion of revenge as nothing is more common in their action than duels or quarrels among the leading characters. "Practices" he says, "that are infamous in reason, capital in law, and damnable in religion, are to the credit of the stage, and Rage and Resentment, Blood and Barbarity are deified." "What must we say," he continues, "of the more foul representations, of all the impudence in language and gesture, can this stuff be the inclination of ladies? Is vice so entertaining, and do they love to see the stews depicted before them. One would think the dishonor of their own Sex the Discovery of so much lewdness, and the treating of Human Nature so very coarsely could have little satisfaction in it." . . . Call you this Diversion? Can Profaneness be such an irresistible Delight? . . . Is the Scorn of Christianity the Entertainment of Christians? Is it such a pleasure to hear the Scriptures burlesqued? Is Ribaldry so very obliging and Atheism so charming a Quality? Are we indeed willing to quit the Privilege of our Nature; to Surrender our Charter of Immortality and throw up the Pretenses to another Life?" And he winds up his conclusion in these words: "In short: Nothing can be more disserviceable to Probity and religion than the management of the *stage*. It cherishes those Passions, and rewards those Vices which 'tis the business of Reason to discountenance. It strikes at the Root of Principle draws off the Inclinations from Virtue and spoils good Education, 'tis the most effectual means to baffle the Force of Discipline, to emasculate people's Spirits and Debauch their Manners."

It is sufficient to say in answer to all this, that an examination of the history of the English and American stage for the two hundred years that have elapsed since these words were written, shows that it has had no such effect, that it has been a rational source of amusement that has been beneficial and not injurious to society. It is the most attractive of all amusements, and that this attraction, as an amusement, has continued to increase, or, at least, has not diminished, would seem to appear from the number of theaters there is now in London, in New York, in Paris, and in other cities of Europe.

It is notable that plays which combine enjoyment with a healthy moral effect are now very much liked, such as Denman Thompson's " Old Homestead," Mr. Herne's " Shore Acres," and Mr. John Hare's " Pair of Spectacles," and plays of a like character that have within the present period been produced in the city of New York by these three managers, Messrs. Augustin Daly, Dan'l Frohman, and A. M. Palmer; and that a taste in this country has been widely diffused for what is exalted in the drama, is found in the fact that crowded audiences, for a hundred nights consecutively, went to see Edwin Booth perform the principal part in a tragedy of so high a character as Shakespeare's " Hamlet."

Another feature in this history of the last two centuries, and especially since the days of John Kemble, and his distinguished sister, Mrs. Siddons, is that the player is no longer a wandering vagabond, or one looked down upon because his sole vocation in life is to minister to our pleasures, but one who is as much respected as any other member of the community, unless he does something individually to forfeit that respect. No player at the present day has, in respect to his vocation, to exclaim against fortune as Shakespeare did in his 99th sonnet:

> The guilty goddess of my harmful deeds,
> That did not better for my life provide,
> Than public means which public manners breeds,
> Thence comes it that my name receives a brand,
> And almost thence my nature is subdued,
> To what it works in like the dyer's hand.

All this is now completely changed, as is shown conclusively by the circumstance that Sir Henry Irving has been honored by being raised to the dignity of a knight for his eminence as an actor. We are, in this respect, where Greece was when the drama had reached its highest perfection:—when Æschylus, who was an actor as well as dramatist, commanded as an officer on the field of Marathon, where his exploits and those of his brother were so remarkable that they were commemorated by a descriptive painting in the theater of Athens; when Neoptolemus, a celebrated tragic actor, was sent as one of the ambassadors to conclude a treaty of peace with Philip; when Aristo-demus, another great tragic actor, was prominent in the political affairs of his time, was also employed upon an embassy, and, on the proposal of Demosthenes, was honored with a golden crown for his public ser-vices; * and when Æschylus, Euripides, and Sophocles produced those plays that have ever since been the admiration of mankind.

* Smith's "Dictionary," Vol. i, p. 42; Calcraft, 67.

Dr. Franklin wished that he could, after a hundred years, return again to this earth to see what science in the meanwhile had accomplished, and could Collier return after the histrionic experience of the last two centuries, it would be to see how unfounded were his conclusions respecting the theater as an institution, and will ever be among any people while the nation remains in a healthy condition.

In conclusion, we may say of the drama, that with the four other arts of poetry, music, sculpture, and painting, it has been the natural outcome of civilization; that as things that are general have always their exceptions, there may have been races, as the Egyptians appear to have been, who, in the development of their civilization, showed no aptitude or desire for it; that its peculiar attraction is, as Lord Bacon says: "That it brings the past before us as if it were the present;" and as respects the present, that it is what Shakespeare and Addison declared it to be, the mirror of human nature.

DATE DUE